ABOUT THIS BOOK

ABOUT THIS BOOK

This book is written for students following the Pearson Edexcel International GCSE (9–1) History specification and covers one unit of the course. This unit is The Origins and Course of the First World War, 1905–18, one of the Historical Investigations.

The History course has been structured so that teaching and learning can take place in any order, both in the classroom and in any independent learning. The book contains five chapters which match the five areas of content in the specification:

- The alliance system and international rivalry, 1905–14
- The growth of tension in Europe, 1905–14
- The Schlieffen Plan and deadlock on the Western Front
- The war at sea and Gallipoli
- The defeat of Germany

Each chapter is split into multiple sections to break down content into manageable chunks and to ensure full coverage of the specification.

Each chapter features a mix of learning and activities. Sources are embedded throughout to develop your understanding and exam-style questions help you to put learning into practice. Recap pages at the end of each chapter summarise key information and let you check your understanding. Exam guidance pages help you prepare confidently for the exam.

Timeline
Visual representation of events to clarify the order in which they happened.

Learning objectives
Each section starts with a list of what you will learn in it. They are carefully tailored to address key assessment objectives central to the course.

Source
Photos, cartoons and text sources are used to explain events and show you what people from the period said, thought or created, helping you to build your understanding.

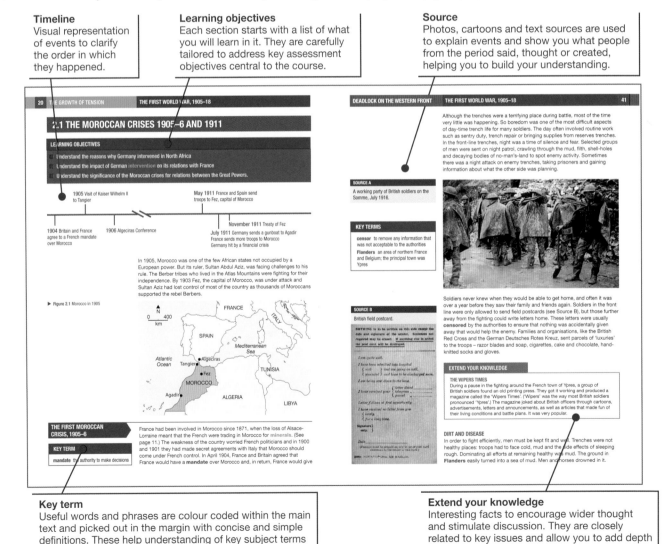

Key term
Useful words and phrases are colour coded within the main text and picked out in the margin with concise and simple definitions. These help understanding of key subject terms and support students whose first language is not English.

Extend your knowledge
Interesting facts to encourage wider thought and stimulate discussion. They are closely related to key issues and allow you to add depth to your knowledge and answers.

Activity
Each chapter includes activities to help check and embed knowledge and understanding.

Recap
At the end of each chapter, you will find a page designed to help you consolidate and reflect on the chapter as a whole.

Recall quiz
This quick quiz is ideal for checking your knowledge or for revision.

Exam-style question
Questions tailored to the Pearson Edexcel specification to allow for practice and development of exam writing technique. They also allow for practice responding to the command words used in the exams.

Skills
Relevant exam questions have been assigned the key skills which you will gain from undertaking them, allowing for a strong focus on particular academic qualities. These transferable skills are highly valued in further study and the workplace.

Hint
All exam-style questions are accompanied by a hint to help you get started on an answer.

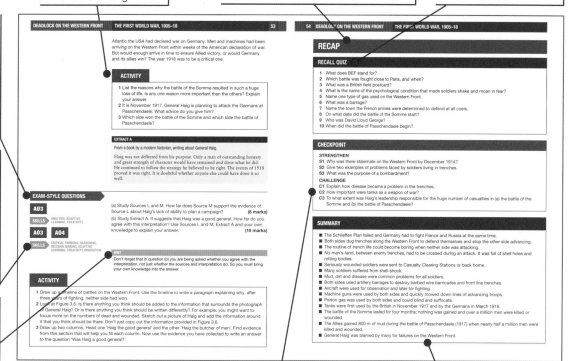

Checkpoint
Checkpoints help you to check and reflect on your learning. The Strengthen section helps you to consolidate knowledge and understanding, and check that you have grasped the basic ideas and skills. The Challenge questions push you to go beyond just understanding the information, and into evaluation and analysis of what you have studied.

Summary
The main points of each chapter are summarised in a series of bullet points. These are great for embedding core knowledge and handy for revision.

Exam guidance
At the end of each chapter, you will find two pages designed to help you better understand the exam questions and how to answer them. Each exam guidance section focuses on a particular question type that you will find in the exam, allowing you to approach them with confidence.

Advice on answering the question
Three key questions about the exam question are answered here in order to explain what the question is testing and what you need to do to succeed in the exam.

Pearson Progression
Sample student answers have been given a Pearson Step from 1 to 12. This tells you how well the response has met the criteria in the Pearson Progression Map.

Commentary
Feedback on the quality of the answer is provided to help you understand their strengths and weaknesses and show how they can be improved.

Student answers
Exemplar student answers are used to show what an answer to the exam question may look like. There are often two levels of answers so you can see what you need to do to write better responses.

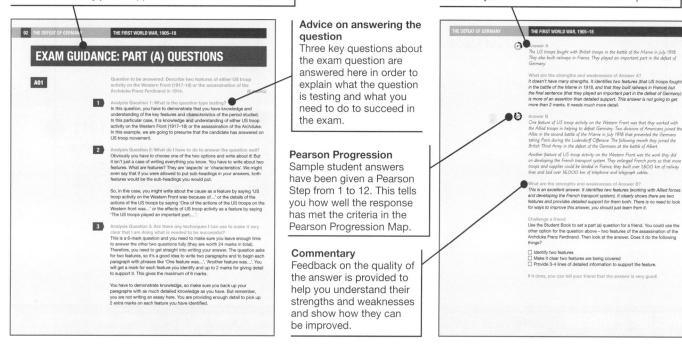

TIMELINE — THE ORIGINS AND COURSE OF THE FIRST WORLD WAR, 1905–18

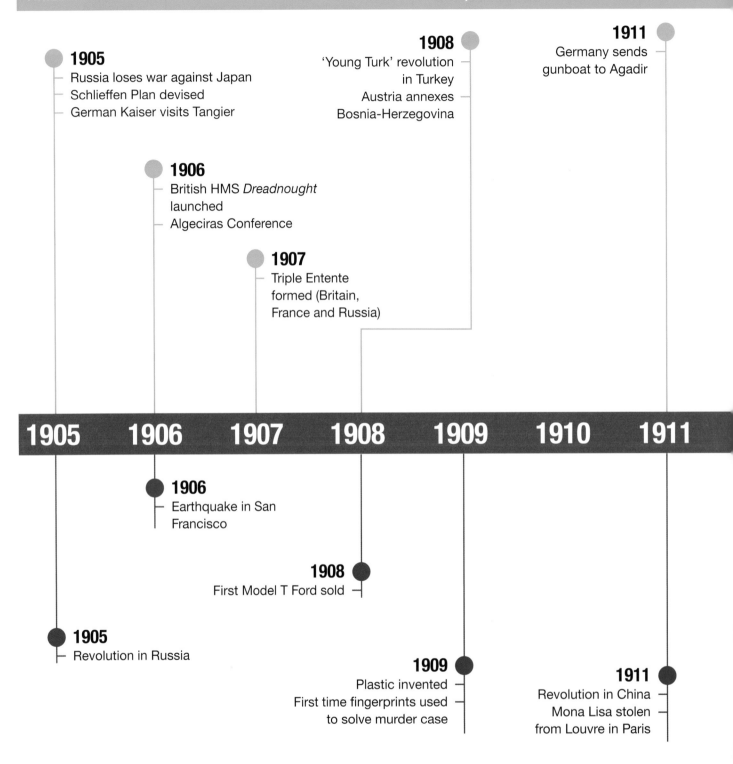

1905
— Russia loses war against Japan
— Schlieffen Plan devised
— German Kaiser visits Tangier

1906
— British HMS *Dreadnought* launched
— Algeciras Conference

1907
— Triple Entente formed (Britain, France and Russia)

1908
'Young Turk' revolution in Turkey —
Austria annexes Bosnia-Herzegovina —

1911
Germany sends gunboat to Agadir

| 1905 | 1906 | 1907 | 1908 | 1909 | 1910 | 1911 |

1906
— Earthquake in San Francisco

1908
First Model T Ford sold —

1905
— Revolution in Russia

1909
Plastic invented —
First time fingerprints used to solve murder case —

1911
Revolution in China —
Mona Lisa stolen from Louvre in Paris —

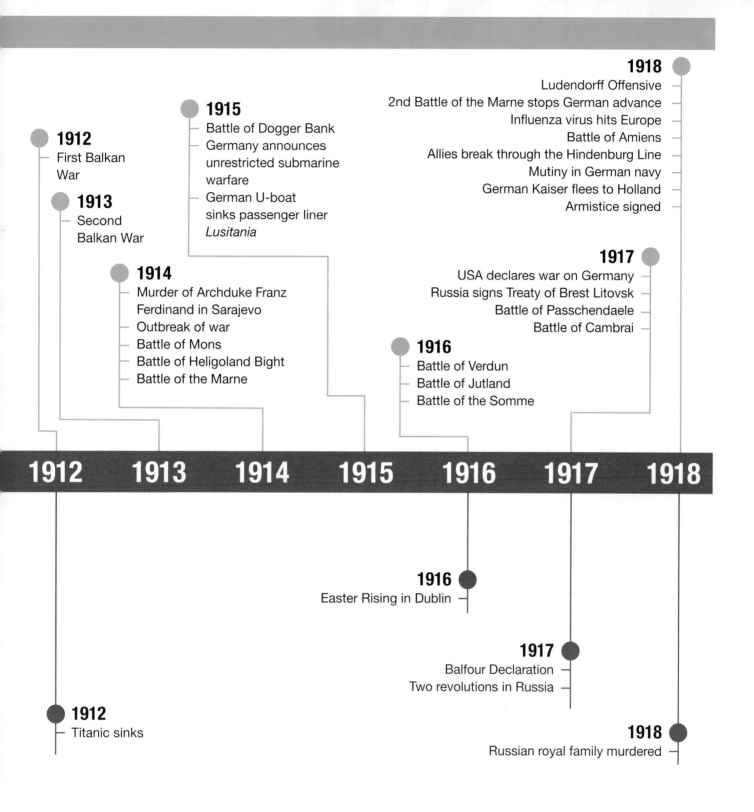

1912
First Balkan War

1913
Second Balkan War

1914
- Murder of Archduke Franz Ferdinand in Sarajevo
- Outbreak of war
- Battle of Mons
- Battle of Heligoland Bight
- Battle of the Marne

1915
- Battle of Dogger Bank
- Germany announces unrestricted submarine warfare
- German U-boat sinks passenger liner *Lusitania*

1916
- Battle of Verdun
- Battle of Jutland
- Battle of the Somme

1917
- USA declares war on Germany
- Russia signs Treaty of Brest Litovsk
- Battle of Passchendaele
- Battle of Cambrai

1918
- Ludendorff Offensive
- 2nd Battle of the Marne stops German advance
- Influenza virus hits Europe
- Battle of Amiens
- Allies break through the Hindenburg Line
- Mutiny in German navy
- German Kaiser flees to Holland
- Armistice signed

1912   1913   1914   1915   1916   1917   1918

1912
- Titanic sinks

1916
- Easter Rising in Dublin

1917
- Balfour Declaration
- Two revolutions in Russia

1918
- Russian royal family murdered

1. THE ALLIANCE SYSTEM AND INTERNATIONAL RIVALRY, 1905–14

LEARNING OBJECTIVES

- Understand the reasons why the Triple Entente was formed
- Understand the significance of imperial and economic rivalry in creating tension between Britain and Germany
- Understand the ways in which an arms race increased tension between the two alliance systems.

In the years after 1905, a mixture of suspicion and fear, ambition and rivalry created enormous tension in Europe. The largest and strongest countries had made alliances with each other so that Europe was divided into two powerful groups. Germany, Austria-Hungary and Italy were in one group; Britain, France and Russia in the other. Rivalry between Britain and Germany over acquiring colonies, and ambitions to become economically the more powerful, increased this division. Nationalism, too, contributed to each group's desire to control international matters. Britain and Germany began strengthening their armies and developing their navies. By 1914, Europe was a dangerous place.

1.1 THE ALLIANCE SYSTEM

LEARNING OBJECTIVES

- Understand why there was tension in Europe in 1905
- Understand the reasons why the Triple Entente was formed
- Understand how the alliance system could be seen by some as a system that kept the peace and by others as making war more likely.

At the beginning of the 20th century there were six 'Great Powers' in Europe. These were Germany, Austria-Hungary, Italy, France, Russia and Great Britain. Although these countries had different aims and ambitions, they had a number of things in common. For example, they all wanted to make sure they were safe from attack and that they had the best opportunity to increase their prosperity by trading in as many overseas markets as possible.

SAFETY IN NUMBERS

In trying to achieve security from attack and increase their opportunities for trade, the Great Powers often found themselves in competition with each other, which had sometimes led to war. By the end of the 19th century they had begun to protect themselves from their rivals by joining together in a system of **alliances**. By 1905, Germany, Austria-Hungary and Italy had formed the Triple Alliance, Russia and France were **allied** in the Franco-Russian Alliance and Britain and France had a friendly agreement called the Entente Cordiale. These alliances reflected which countries considered themselves to have similar aims and who they considered to be their greatest rivals. The tensions between the rival powers that existed in 1905 gradually deepened, until war broke out in 1914.

WHY WAS THERE TENSION IN EUROPE IN 1905?

This topic begins in 1905 and you won't be expected to answer questions in the exam on events before then. But there are a few things you do need to know about to help you understand the tensions existing in 1905. One of those is the reasons why some countries were rivals with others.

GERMANY

Germany was a new country, formed following **unification** of the German states in 1871, after the Germans had defeated France in the Franco-Prussian war. As part of the **peace treaty** after the war, Germany took Alsace-Lorraine from France. This was an important industrial area. German politicians were afraid that the French might attack Germany to get Alsace-Lorraine back. So Germany and France were rivals.

AUSTRIA-HUNGARY

Austria-Hungary was a large **empire** in central Europe. It contained people of many different nationalities, some of whom wanted independence. Serbia was already an independent country and there were Serbs living in Austria-Hungary who wanted to join with Serbia. The main concern of the Austrian emperor was to keep the empire together, but Russia supported the Serbs and so Austria-Hungary and Russia were rivals.

▶ **Figure 1.1** Europe in 1905

Unified in 1871, Kaiser Wilhelm II ruled over a country of 68 million people. Since 1871, Germany had industrialised rapidly and was a highly successful industrial and technological country, with most people living in towns. The German Kaiser and the British King George V were cousins.

The tsar, Nicholas II, ruled over the largest, and one of the poorest, countries in the world. It was an empire of many different peoples who spoke different languages. Much of the land was not farmed because it was too cold. There was little industry. For a large part of each year, Russian ports could not operate because the sea was frozen.

The head of state was King Edward VII and the prime minister was Arthur Balfour. Britain had been the first country in the world to industrialise, and well over half of the population of 46 million people lived in towns. Industry prospered and trade flourished.

The president of France, Emile Loubet, governed a country the size of Germany, containing 40 million people. The birth rate had fallen and the population was ageing. Although there was industry in the north-east, France was largely a rural country.

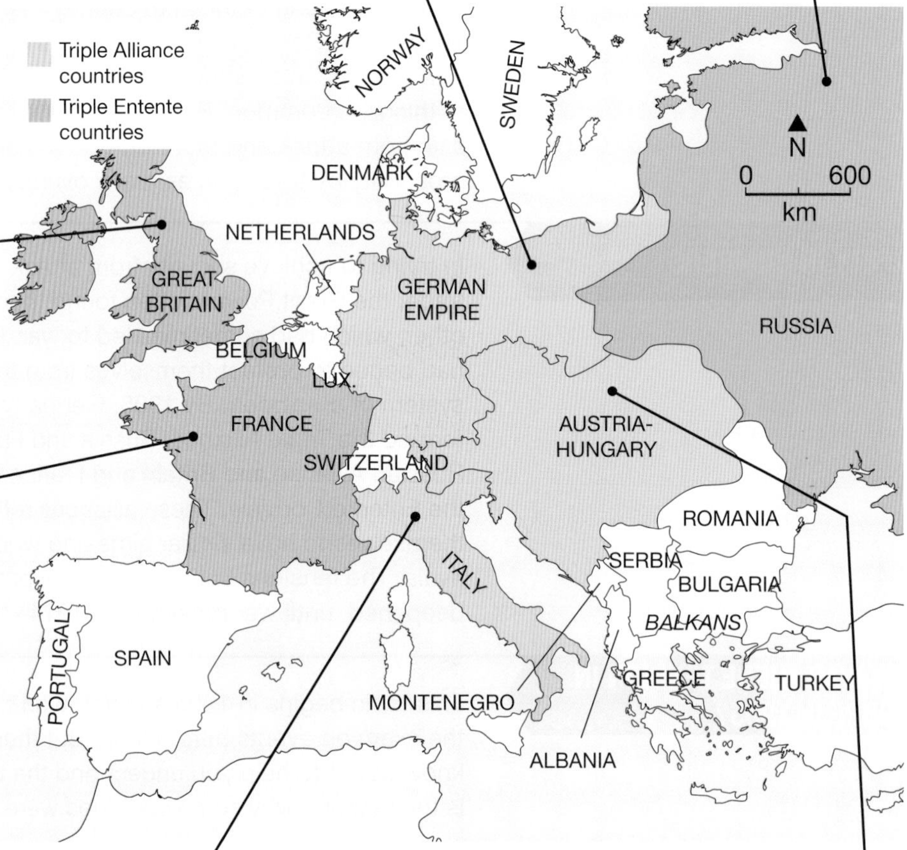

Italy was unified in 1871, although a large number of Italians remained in Austria-Hungary after unification. Italy was a constitutional monarchy, and the king, Victor Emmanuel III, ruled over 35 million people. Although mainly an agricultural country, there was considerable industry in the northern areas.

The emperor, Franz-Joseph, ruled over 50 million people in a country with little heavy industry. His people were divided into at least 11 different nationalities, including Magyars, Czechs, Slovaks, Serbs, Croats and Slavs. Each had its own language and way of life.

Triple Alliance countries

Triple Entente countries

NORWAY
SWEDEN
DENMARK
NETHERLANDS
GREAT BRITAIN
BELGIUM
LUX.
GERMAN EMPIRE
RUSSIA
FRANCE
SWITZERLAND
AUSTRIA-HUNGARY
ROMANIA
ITALY
SERBIA
BULGARIA
BALKANS
PORTUGAL
SPAIN
GREECE
TURKEY
MONTENEGRO
ALBANIA

N
0   600
km

ITALY

Italy was another new country, which had been formed in 1861. It was not a strong industrial or military power, and so it wanted to ally with other countries to make itself more powerful. When Italy joined Germany and Austria-Hungary in the Triple Alliance in 1882, it became part of an anti-France, anti-Russia alliance.

FRANCE

France's main concern in 1905 was to make sure that it would never again be attacked by Germany and to get Alsace-Lorraine back. France allied with Russia in 1892 because it wanted support against Germany.

RUSSIA

Russia was the largest of the six powers, but the least developed. Russia's main concerns were that Germany would expand into Russian territory in central Europe and that Austria-Hungary would take measures against **Slavs** in Austria-Hungary (Russians and Serbians were both Slav peoples).

GREAT BRITAIN

During the 19th century, Britain had tried not to get involved in European politics. This policy was known as '**splendid isolation**'. British had a powerful navy and overseas empire and didn't see a need to form alliances with European countries. But by the beginning of the 20th century, the German Kaiser had shown that he wanted Germany to have an empire and a strong navy, which was a direct threat to the British Empire and its naval dominance. So in 1904 Britain joined with France in the Entente Cordiale.

SOURCE A

A French cartoon published in 1913. It shows a French boy looking down on the lost regions of Alsace-Lorraine. Above him in the skies gallop the ghosts of French cavalrymen killed in the Franco-Prussian war, 1870–71.

So, even as early as 1905, Europe was beginning to divide into two separate groups whose rivalry would lead to war in 1914. Why did the tensions that existed in 1905 worsen to the point that the Great Powers had to go to war?

In 1907 Russia joined the **entente**, making it a Triple Entente. There was no formal agreement to go to help each other if one of them was attacked. However, it was agreed that they had a **moral obligation** to support each other.

EXTEND YOUR KNOWLEDGE

COUSINS BECOME ENEMIES
King George V of Great Britain and Kaiser Wilhelm II of Germany were cousins. They had the same grandmother, the British Queen Victoria. The King's father, Edward, and the Kaiser's mother, Victoria, were brother and sister.

SOURCE B

From *The Times*, a British newspaper, April 1914.

The division of the Great Powers into two well-balanced groups is a two-fold check upon unreasonable ambitions or a sudden outbreak of race hatred. All monarchs and statesmen – and all nations – know that a war of group against group would be an enormous disaster. They are no longer answerable only to themselves.

SOURCE C

A British cartoon of Kaiser Wilhelm II in his bath. He is reaching for a piece of soap shaped like Europe. The cartoon was printed on a postcard in 1914.

HE WONT BE HAPPY TILL HE GETS IT

EUROPE

EXTEND YOUR KNOWLEDGE

KAISER WILHELM II
Despite being born with a withered left arm, Wilhelm became an excellent horseman. He could swim, hunt, shoot and fence. He loved the army and enjoyed dressing up in military uniforms.

ACTIVITY

1 Draw a table with three columns. Head the columns, starting from the left, 'Great Powers', 'Fear' and 'Ambition'. In the 'Great Powers' column, list the six Great Powers. In the other two columns, write what each power was afraid of, and what each power wanted.
2 Keep the table and add to it as you work through this chapter. By the end of the chapter, you will have a very good idea why war broke out in 1914.
3 Look at Source A. What is the message of the cartoon?
4 Look at Sources A and C. Work with a partner.
   a One of you should make a list of the points each artist is making. The other should look at the cartoons from the German point of view.
   b List the points that a German person could find threatening.
   c Share your ideas with the rest of your class.

EXAM-STYLE QUESTION

A01

Describe **two** features of the alliance system in 1905.   **(6 marks)**

HINT

You need to identify two features of the alliance system – so don't just say who is on each side!

1.2 EMPIRES AND ECONOMICS

LEARNING OBJECTIVES

☐ Understand why colonial rivalry led to strained relations among the European powers

☐ Understand how economic rivalries created international tensions

☐ Understand the relative strengths of the Great Powers in 1914.

The desire to acquire **colonies**, mainly shown by Germany, disturbed Britain and France, which already had large overseas colonial empires. People were generally very proud of their empires and expressed this in various **patriotic** ways that added to the growth of tension in Europe. Colonies provided **raw materials** and were markets for goods produced by the European powers that governed them. In this way the colonies were linked to the strength of different European countries. The people of Britain and France put pressure on their governments if they felt these empires were under threat.

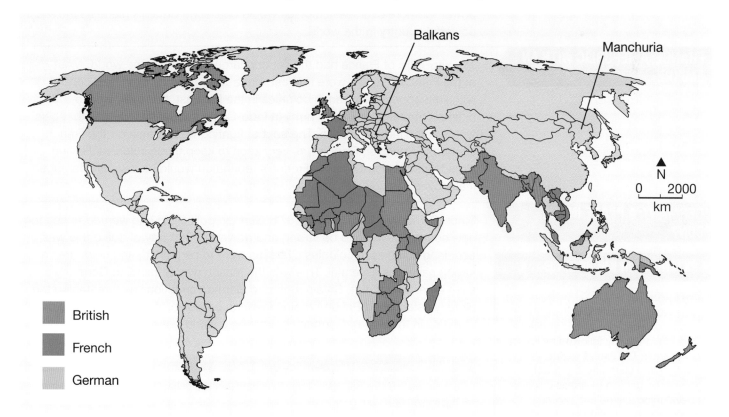

British

French

German

▲ Figure 1.2 The European powers and their overseas colonies in 1914

IMPERIAL RIVALRY

KEY TERM

imperial relating to an empire

EXTEND YOUR KNOWLEDGE

THE SCRAMBLE FOR AFRICA
The Scramble for Africa refers to the rush by European powers to gain colonies in Africa. In 1870, 10 per cent of Africa was under European control. By 1914, this had risen to 90 per cent.

The European powers were all involved in trying to win, or supporting, colonies. This led to **imperial** rivalry between the Great Powers to see who could get the largest empire. Some of the Great Powers, like Russia and Austria-Hungary, were hoping to expand on mainland Europe. Others, like Great Britain, France and Germany, focused on countries outside Europe. The European powers believed that they had the right to run other countries. They did this usually by invading and simply taking over, or by being given a country as part of a treaty arrangement.

GREAT BRITAIN: AN OVERSEAS EMPIRE

Great Britain is a small island country off the coast of Europe. In 1905, it was the most powerful country in the world. This was partly because of its vast overseas empire (see Figure 1.2). The British Empire took up nearly a quarter of the world's land surface area and a quarter of the world's population lived in the British Empire under its control. It was important that Britain kept in close contact with its colonies. This was partly because of the need to control and to manage them, and partly because of the need to trade with them. India, for example, supplied raw cotton to Britain, and Britain exported cotton cloth to India. In the days before air travel, this contact was maintained by sea. Merchant ships sailed the sea routes to the British colonies and the Royal Navy kept the sea routes open and clear of enemy shipping. Any challenge to the navy would endanger the security of the empire. Any push by a European power for more overseas colonies would challenge Britain's place as the most powerful country in the world.

FRANCE: A REPUBLIC WITH AN EMPIRE

The republic of France had the second largest empire in the world. Most of the French colonies were in West Africa where France exercised control with little opposition. French colonies in the Far East, however, were a different matter. The French army in Indo-China frequently fought with rebels who wanted independence. The cost of fighting was a strain on the French economy. However, France was very keen to keep those colonies. Having already lost Alsace-Lorraine, France's reputation would be severely damaged if any overseas colonies were to be lost, too.

GERMANY: A PLACE IN THE SUN?

EXTEND YOUR KNOWLEDGE

WELTPOLITIK
The word 'weltpolitik' is the German word for world policy. It is applied to the foreign policy followed by Kaiser Wilhelm II. The aim of weltpolitik was to turn Germany into a world power by gaining overseas colonies, developing a large and powerful navy, and negotiating in a forceful way in international affairs.

Since Germany's formation in 1871, German politicians had wanted to see the new country develop to be strong and powerful. One way of doing this was by acquiring colonies. If colonies overseas were to be gained, and held, then a strong navy was essential. This was the reason why Britain and Germany saw each other as a threat. Britain regarded German ambitions as threatening the already established British Empire; German politicians came to see Britain as standing in the way of Germany becoming a world power.

SOURCE D

From a speech by the German Foreign Secretary during a debate in the German parliament, 6 December 1897.

We wish to throw no one into the shade, but we demand our own place in the sun.

THE EUROPEAN POWERS AND THEIR OVERSEAS COLONIES IN 1914

	▼ GREAT BRITAIN	▼ FRANCE	▼ RUSSIA	▼ GERMANY	▼ AUSTRIA-HUNGARY
Population	40.8 million	39.6 million	159 million	65 million	50 million
Population of colonies	390 million	58 million	0	15 million	0
Number of colonies	56	29	0	10	0
Size of colonies	27 million sq km	11 million sq km	0	2.5 million sq km	0

RUSSIA AND AUSTRIA-HUNGARY: LAND-BASED EMPIRES?

KEY TERM

Balkans a large area in south-east Europe that includes Albania, Bosnia and Herzegovina, Bulgaria, Greece, Kosova, Macedonia, Montenegro, Serbia and Turkey

Neither Russia nor Austria-Hungary had overseas empires, nor did they want them. Russia wanted to expand within Europe, and Austria-Hungary wanted to control the different nationalities within its borders and so become strong.

■ Russia (see Figure 1.1) stretched from the Baltic Sea in the west to the Bering Strait in the east. Russia wanted to expand south-east into Manchuria in order to have ice-free ports. Russia also wanted to expand into the **Balkans** so that Russian ships would have access to the Mediterranean Sea and, by sailing through the Strait of Gibraltar, to the Atlantic Ocean.

■ Austria-Hungary (see Figure 1.1) was a union of two separate countries: Austria and Hungary. Franz-Joseph ruled an empire containing 11 different nationalities. The government was struggling to hold them together in one empire. For example, a move to force all Czechs to use German – the language of Austria – in schools and workplaces led to riots. Austria-Hungary was afraid, too, that the Serbs within its borders might want to break away and join Serbia.

ACTIVITY

1 Read Source D. What did the German Foreign Secretary mean by 'our own place in the sun'?
2 Set up a debate. One side must argue that Germany had a right to possess more colonies; the other side must argue that Germany had no such right. You could use the information in the table above as part of the argument.
3 Write a report of the debate for a local newspaper. Make it as exciting as you can.

NATIONALISM

Nationalism is very closely linked to empire and imperialism. Nationalism, the love of one's country, is usually considered to be positive. Loyalty to the same set of values and beliefs is what unites the people of a country. However, when nationalism becomes too strong, and the supporters of a country too extreme in their support, nationalism becomes aggressive.

It was the build-up of nationalism in the years to 1914 that helped to prepare people for war and inspired young men to join up and fight.

SOURCE E

This is the chorus from a British patriotic song, written in 1902.

Land of hope and glory, mother of the free,
How shall we extol thee, who are born of thee?
Wider still and wider shall thy bounds be set.
God, who made thee mighty, make thee mightier yet.
God, who made thee mighty, make thee mightier yet.

SOURCE F

This is a traditional German patriotic song, first used at official ceremonies after 1890. It later became the German national anthem.

Germany, Germany above all else,
Above all else in the world,
When, for protection and defence,
It always stands brotherly together.
From the Meuse to the Memel,
From the Adige to the Belt,
Germany, Germany above all else,
Above all else in the world!

SOURCE G

A British First World War recruitment poster.

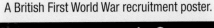

YOUR COUNTRY'S CALL

Isn't this worth fighting for?
ENLIST NOW

ACTIVITY

Read Sources E and F.
1 Use a dictionary to look up words you don't know. How can you tell that these are patriotic songs?
2 Pick out the line in each song that is the most patriotic.
  a Discuss with a partner the similarities and differences between the songs.
  b Which song appeals more strongly to nationalist feelings?
3 Look at Source G. Not many people lived in villages like the one in the poster. Why would the British government use this image?

ECONOMIC RIVALRY

The wealth of a country is very important when there are international disagreements. If a country is wealthy, it has money to build an army or navy to protect itself. A country becomes wealthy through economic activity, such as buying and selling goods. If a country is rich in raw materials and has efficient industry and markets to sell its goods to, it will become wealthy. At the beginning of the 20th century there was increasing rivalry between the European powers to have the major share of economic activity in Europe. This increased tension between the Great Powers.

GREAT BRITAIN V GERMANY

Britain was the first country in the world to industrialise. British-manufactured goods flooded the markets in Europe and the British Empire. Britain took many different raw materials from its empire. The British economy became strong, and in the 19th century Britain was the richest country in Europe. However, after unification, Germany began to industrialise very quickly. German manufacturers modernised **machinery** that had been invented in Britain and

SOURCE H

An advertisement for electric light, published by a British company in about 1900.

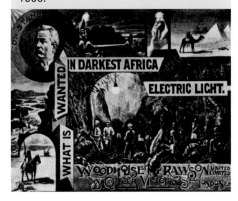

made manufacturing processes more efficient. By 1890, German manufactured goods were competing with British ones in all the markets that had previously been dominated by Britain. German merchant ships competed with British merchant ships to carry goods around the world. By 1914, Germany was producing more iron, steel, coal – and even cars – than Britain. Britain's economic lead had gone. Germany had taken over from Great Britain as the strongest power, economically.

FRANCE V GERMANY

When France lost Alsace-Lorraine to Germany, it had to import coal from other countries. This seriously weakened the French economy because of the cost involved. France began to explore the possibilities of mining minerals in Morocco. These could be used in agriculture and industry but would also bring France into competition with Germany. This was because Germany was afraid that France was trying to turn Morocco into a French colony.

RUSSIA V GERMANY AND AUSTRIA-HUNGARY

Germany and Austria-Hungary had well-established commercial markets in the Balkans. In 1888, Russia had begun to build a railway in the area. Germany and Austria-Hungary regarded this as a threat because a railway would allow Russian-produced goods to be transported to the area more easily. Even though Russia had not yet fully industrialised and had little by way of manufactured goods to export, Germany and Austria-Hungary were worried about what might happen in the future.

THE EUROPEAN POWERS AND THEIR ECONOMIES IN 1914

	▽ GREAT BRITAIN	▽ FRANCE	▽ RUSSIA	▽ GERMANY	▽ AUSTRIA-HUNGARY
Coal produced	292 million tonnes	40 million tonnes	36.2 million tonnes	277 million tonnes	47 million tonnes
Steel produced	11 million tonnes	4.6 million tonnes	3.6 million tonnes	14 million tonnes	5 million tonnes

ACTIVITY

1 Look at Source H. How is the British company using the British colonies in Africa to advertise electric light, the product they are selling?

2 Using the information in the tables on page 9 and on this page, create a histogram (bar chart) that summarises the information for each country.
 a Which European power, using just the information on your histogram, is the strongest? Why?
 b Which European power, using just the information on your histogram, is the weakest? Why?

3 Draw two circles. Label one 'Colonies' and the other 'European powers'.
 a Draw links between them that show how, economically, they are useful to each other.
 b In your own words, explain how economic strength and colonies are linked.

4 You have now finished this section. Go back to the grid you started in answer to question 1 at the end of Section 1.1. Now add to it, using the information in this section.

1.3 MILITARY RIVALRY: PLANNING FOR WAR?

LEARNING OBJECTIVES

- Understand the impact of Anglo-German naval rivalry on increasing tension in Europe
- Understand the significance of planning for a war on land
- Understand the reasons why military rivalry took Europe to the edge of war.

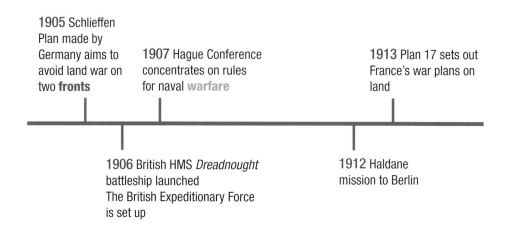

1905 Schlieffen Plan made by Germany aims to avoid land war on two **fronts**

1906 British HMS *Dreadnought* battleship launched
The British Expeditionary Force is set up

1907 Hague Conference concentrates on rules for naval **warfare**

1912 Haldane mission to Berlin

1913 Plan 17 sets out France's war plans on land

KEY TERM

front the area where fighting happens in a war

Tensions increased in Europe over military matters. Germany grew ever more afraid of being surrounded by hostile countries. British politicians came to believe that Germany was aiming at European, and possibly world, domination. There was fear and suspicion on both sides, especially between Germany and Britain. Britain wanted to remain the most powerful country, but Germany was pressing for change.

THE NAVAL RACE

Britain relied on its massive navy to keep the sea routes open to the furthest parts of its empire, and to protect its economic interests and the people there. The navy was essential, too, to protect Britain, an island nation, against any European **aggression**. However, there were people in Germany, including the Kaiser, who believed that if Germany were to become a world power with a large empire, it had to challenge the might of the British navy.

- In 1898 and 1900, Germany passed the Navy Laws. The first one gave permission for the building of 16 battleships; the second increased this number to 46. There were to be 60 **cruisers**, too. So by 1905 Germany had begun to build more battleships and cruisers. The German naval chief, Admiral Tirpitz, set up the Naval League. This was intended to encourage the German people to take an interest in their navy. Tours of German ports were organised, and lectures about the naval **fleet** were given all over Germany.
- The British response was to build the best ever battleship – HMS *Dreadnought*. Launched in 1906, it was so advanced that its revolutionary design made all other battleships instantly out-of-date. The ship gave its name, Dreadnought, to a whole class of battleships.

SOURCE I

From a paper written for the British cabinet by the First Lord of the Admiralty in October 1902.

The more the composition of the new German High Seas Fleet is examined, the clearer it becomes that it is designed for a possible conflict with the British Grand Fleet. It cannot be designed for the purpose of playing a leading part in a future war between Germany and France and Russia. A war between France and Russia can only be decided by armies on land.

- Germany responded by building *Rheinland*, their own version of HMS *Dreadnought*. Britain's naval chief, Admiral Fisher, immediately ordered the building of a 'super-Dreadnought', HMS *Neptune*.
- Hundreds of men were recruited by both Germany and Britain and trained as sailors on the new battleships.

The race was on. Between 1906 and 1914, Britain built 29 Dreadnoughts; Germany built 17.

HMS *DREADNOUGHT*

What was so different about HMS *Dreadnought*? The battleship was faster and more heavily armoured than any other warship, and was designed to fight at a distance. The ship could carry 800 sailors and could travel at 22 knots. The armour was about 28 cm thick on the sides and 35 cm thick on the decks. The huge guns could turn and fire shells further than any earlier ship, and could blow up an enemy ship that was 32 km away. This made ships with smaller guns ineffective because they would never be able to get close enough to fire their guns before they were blown up in the water.

SOURCE J

A Dreadnought class battleship, HMS *Iron Duke*, leading a long line of British warships in 1914.

EXTEND YOUR KNOWLEDGE

FEAR OF HMS *DREADNOUGHT*
German sailors began to call their ships 'Five Minute Ships' because they thought that five minutes was all that it would take HMS *Dreadnought* to sink them.

THE ARMS RACE ON LAND

The arms race was not just confined to ships and navies. All the European powers were building their armies and armaments.

- Russia's defeat in the Russo-Japanese war of 1905 led the Russian government to change the way the army was organised. A State Defence Council was formed. This dealt with such things as war plans and the intelligence service. The new Main Directorate of General Staff dealt with recruitment and training the soldiers. However, the Russian army was badly equipped even though it was huge.
- Austria-Hungary began secretly making enormous cannons in their Skoda works.

KEY TERM

mobilise when a country prepares its army to fight a war

- In 1906, the British War Minister, Richard Haldane, formed a British Expeditionary Force of 144,000 soldiers who could travel immediately to France in support of French troops if a war was declared. He created a **Territorial Army** of **volunteers** to back up the regular forces. He set up an Officer Training Corps in schools so that older boys could train to be officers.
- Germany and France made war plans. They needed to work out in advance how they would fight their enemies if ever it became necessary.

▼ Figure 1.3 The Schlieffen Plan

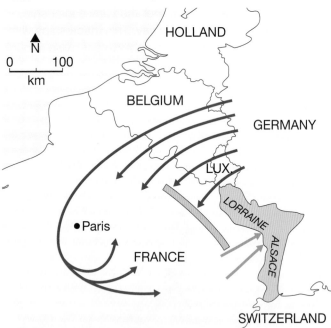

→ Advance of troops according to the Schlieffen Plan

→ Advance troops according to Plan 17

▨ Line of French fortresses

▨ Area lost to Germany in 1871

THE SCHLIEFFEN PLAN

The Schlieffen Plan was created in December 1905 by Count Alfred von Schlieffen. He was the most senior general in the German army. He knew that on land, Germany's two main enemies were France and Russia. In working out a war plan, he had to face the possibility that Germany would have to fight a war on two fronts – against Russia in the east and France in the west – at the same time. No general likes to do this because he can only use half his army against each enemy. It was essential that Schlieffen found a way round this.

Schlieffen believed that Russia, because it was so large and had poor road and rail systems, would probably take about 6 weeks to **mobilise**. This would give the German army extra time. He planned that the German army would first attack and defeat France. They would invade France by travelling at high speed through Belgium and northern France, and attack Paris. Once Paris was captured, France would surrender. The German army could then turn to face Russia. It was a simple plan, but it didn't quite turn out like that. (See Chapter 3.)

PLAN 17

The need to take Alsace-Lorraine back under French control dominated French military thinking. In 1913, the French army chief, General Joffre, came up with Plan 17, which was even simpler than the Schlieffen Plan. In the event of a war breaking out, French troops would immediately make an all-out attack on Alsace-Lorraine. They would successfully capture these two provinces, making them part of France again. Then French troops would cross the River Rhine and advance on Berlin. After years of planning, this was the only strategy the French had developed.

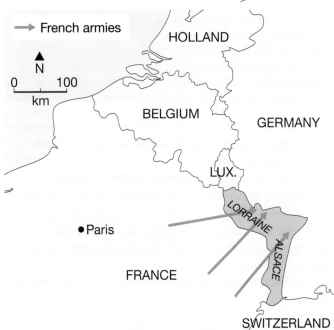

◀ Figure 1.4 Plan 17

EXAM-STYLE QUESTION

A01

Describe **two** features of the naval race.   **(6 marks)**

> **HINT**
>
> You need to identify two different features of the naval race. Don't just say what they were; add a sentence or two of supporting information.

TRYING TO REACH AGREEMENTS

The arms race made Europe a dangerous place, but it did not automatically lead to war.

■ At the end of the previous century, to try to prevent war, a Permanent Court of Arbitration had been set up, but taking disputes to the court was voluntary.

■ In February 1912, Richard Haldane, the British War Minister, made a secret visit to Berlin. Haldane hoped to persuade the Germans to accept voluntary limitation on the arms race. He failed.

So tension between the Great Powers remained high. All it would take was a serious crisis for the tension to tip over into war.

ACTIVITY

1 Work with a partner. Look carefully at the Schlieffen Plan (see Figure 1.3) and list the problems with this plan. Now look at Plan 17. How likely is it that Plan 17 would stop the Schlieffen Plan from working?

2 Did the arms race make war more, or less, likely?

   a Working with a partner, draw up two lists – one with all the reasons why the alliance system made war more likely, and the other with all the reasons why the alliance system made war less likely.

   b Compare your lists with others in your class. Can you reach a conclusion with which you all agree?

3 Use the information in this section to complete the grid on which you have been working. Keep it in your file because you will need it to answer a more wide-ranging question at the end of the next chapter.

▼ Figure 1.5 Who had what in 1914?

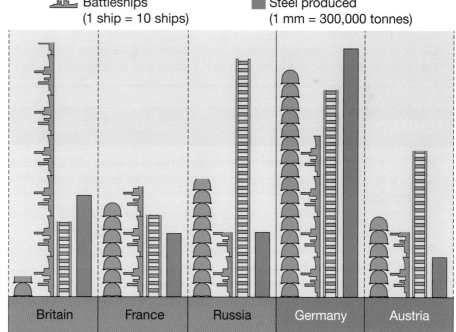

Soldiers available
(1 hat = 500,000 soldiers)

Battleships
(1 ship = 10 ships)

Kilometres of railway track
(1 rung = 16,000 km)

Steel produced
(1 mm = 300,000 tonnes)

Britain   France   Russia   Germany   Austria

RECAP

RECALL QUIZ

1 In what year was the Triple Entente formed?
2 Who were the members of the Triple Entente?
3 Which two provinces did France want to regain from Germany?
4 What was the name of the German Kaiser?
5 Why did Germany want colonies?
6 How big was the British Empire?
7 Why was the navy important to Great Britain?
8 When was HMS *Dreadnought* launched?
9 What was the name of the German war plan?
10 What was Plan 17?

CHECKPOINT

STRENGTHEN

S1 Why were the Triple Alliance and the Triple Entente formed?
S2 Give two examples of the reasons why colonies were important to the Great Powers.
S3 What was the arms race?

CHALLENGE

C1 Explain how the alliance system could be seen as (a) maintaining peace in Europe and (b) making a European war more likely.
C2 How important was economic rivalry in increasing tensions between the Great Powers?
C3 To what extent did the arms race turn Europe into a dangerous place?

SUMMARY

■ A Triple Entente was formed between Britain and France (1904) and Russia (1907).
■ The two alliance systems clashed over a number of different issues. The countries in both systems were suspicious of each other.
■ Germany wanted an empire, and Britain and France saw this as a threat to their own overseas empires. This led to the growth of nationalism in Britain and European countries.
■ German-manufactured goods competed with British ones in markets that had previously been dominated by Britain. Britain saw this as a threat to their economy.
■ Germany began expanding its navy. Britain saw this as a threat to the British navy, which was needed to keep open the sea routes to its empire. A naval race began between Britain and Germany to see which country could build the most warships.
■ All European powers, including Britain, began building up their arms and armaments.
■ The Schlieffen Plan was developed as the German war plan. It aimed to avoid Germany having to fight a war against France and Russia at the same time. The plan was to defeat France quickly by a rapid invasion through Belgium before turning to fight Russia, a country Germany believed would take a long time to mobilise.
■ Plan 17 was the French war plan. French armies would first re-take Alsace-Lorraine, provinces France had lost to Germany in a war in 1870, and would then invade Germany.
■ By 1914, Europe was a dangerous place.

EXAM GUIDANCE: PART (A) QUESTIONS

AO1

Question to be answered: Describe two features of either the Schlieffen Plan (1905) or the Battle of the Somme (1916). (6 marks)

1 **Analysis Question 1: What is the question type testing?**
In this question, you have to demonstrate that you have knowledge and understanding of the key features and characteristics of the period studied. In this particular case, it is knowledge and understanding of either the Schlieffen Plan or the Battle of the Somme. In this example, we are going to presume that the candidate has answered on the Schlieffen Plan, because you won't be studying the Battle of the Somme until Chapter 3.

2 **Analysis Question 2: What do I have to do to answer the question well?**
Obviously you have to choose one of the two options and write about it! But it isn't just a case of writing everything you know. You have to write about two features. What are features? They are 'aspects' or 'characteristics'. We might even say that, if you were allowed to put sub-headings in your answers, both features would be the sub-headings you would put.

So, in this case, you might write about the details of the Schlieffen Plan as a feature by saying 'The Schlieffen Plan was…', or the effects of the Schlieffen Plan as a feature by saying 'The Schlieffen Plan was a failure because…'.

3 **Analysis Question 3: Are there any techniques I can use to make it very clear that I am doing what is needed to be successful?**
This is a 6-mark question and you need to make sure you leave enough time to answer the other two questions fully (they are worth 24 marks in total). Therefore, you need to get straight into writing your answer. The question asks for two features, so it's a good idea to write two paragraphs and to begin each paragraph with phrases like 'One feature was…'; 'Another feature was…'. You will get a mark for each feature you identify and up to 2 marks for giving detail to support it. This gives the maximum of 6 marks.

You have to demonstrate knowledge, so make sure you back up your paragraphs with as much detailed knowledge as you have. But remember, you are not writing an essay here. You are providing enough detail to pick up 2 extra marks on each feature you have identified.

Answer A

The Schlieffen Plan was a plan to fight two of Germany's enemies, France and Russia. It planned not to fight them at the same time. The Plan failed.

What are the strengths and weaknesses of Answer A?
It doesn't have many strengths. It identifies a feature (the Plan was to attack France and Germany) but the second sentence (it planned not to fight them at the same time) is correct but does not say how this was to be done and so cannot count as detailed support. The fact that the Plan failed could be another feature, but lacks detail as to why. So this answer is not going to get more than 2 marks. It needs much more detail.

Answer B

One feature of the Schlieffen Plan was that it aimed to avoid Germany having to fight a war on two fronts. Russia and France were Germany's two enemies on mainland Europe, and if Germany had to fight them at the same time, Germany's army would have to be divided in two, with one half fighting on the frontier with Russia and the other half fighting on the frontier with France. This was not likely to lead to victory for Germany.

Another feature of the Schlieffen Plan was that in order for it to work, it assumed that Russia would be slow to mobilise. This meant that the Plan was to attack France first and win before having to turn and fight Russia. The Plan failed because Belgian troops delayed the German army as it advanced towards France. This meant that France wasn't defeated quickly. Russia mobilised more quickly than the Plan anticipated, and so Germany had, in the end, to fight a war on two fronts. This Plan had failed because this is what it had been written to avoid.

What are the strengths and weaknesses of Answer B?
This is an excellent answer. It identifies two features (what the Schlieffen Plan was written to avoid and that it failed). It clearly shows there are two features and provides detailed support for them both. There is no need to look for ways to improve this answer, you should just learn from it.

Challenge a friend
Use the Student Book to set a part (a) question for a friend. You might choose The Triple Entente or rivalry between the Great Powers. Then look at the answer. Does it do the following things?

☐ Identify two features
☐ Make it clear two features are being covered
☐ Provide 3-4 lines of detailed information to support the feature.

If it does, you can tell your friend that the answer is very good!

2. THE GROWTH OF TENSION IN EUROPE, 1905–14

LEARNING OBJECTIVES

☐ Understand the impact of Anglo-German rivalry in North Africa on the increasing tension between the European powers

☐ Understand the significance of conflict in the Balkans for increasing tension in Eastern Europe

☐ Understand why the assassination of Archduke Franz Ferdinand in Sarajevo led to the outbreak of war in 1914.

The European powers had created a dangerous situation by forming alliances and making plans for war against each other. As the arms race grew, the more nervous and suspicious the different countries became. Two serious disputes occurred, one in the Balkans and one in North Africa. Austria-Hungary clashed with Russia as they both wanted to control the Balkans. In North Africa, France and Britain clashed with Germany, which opposed French control of Morocco. Both these disputes were so serious that they could have led to war. This didn't happen, but the quarrels increased tensions in Europe almost to breaking point. The flash point came in the Balkans in June 1914. Archduke Franz Ferdinand, heir to the Austro-Hungarian throne, was assassinated. Less than 2 months later, Europe exploded into war.

2.1 THE MOROCCAN CRISES 1905–6 AND 1911

LEARNING OBJECTIVES

- ☐ Understand the reasons why Germany intervened in North Africa
- ☐ Understand the impact of German **intervention** on its relations with France
- ☐ Understand the significance of the Moroccan crises for relations between the Great Powers.

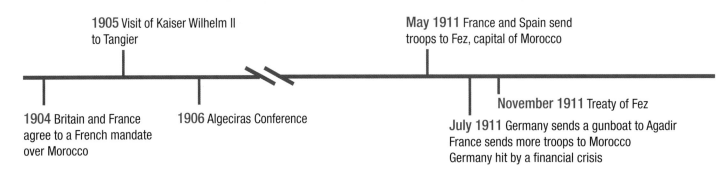

1905 Visit of Kaiser Wilhelm II to Tangier

May 1911 France and Spain send troops to Fez, capital of Morocco

1904 Britain and France agree to a French mandate over Morocco

1906 Algeciras Conference

November 1911 Treaty of Fez

July 1911 Germany sends a gunboat to Agadir France sends more troops to Morocco Germany hit by a financial crisis

In 1905, Morocco was one of the few African states not occupied by a European power. But its ruler, Sultan Abdul Aziz, was facing challenges to his rule. The Berber tribes who lived in the Atlas Mountains were fighting for their independence. By 1903 Fez, the capital of Morocco, was under attack and Sultan Aziz had lost control of most of the country as thousands of Moroccans supported the rebel Berbers.

▶ **Figure 2.1** Morocco in 1905

THE FIRST MOROCCAN CRISIS, 1905–6

KEY TERM

mandate the authority to make decisions

France had been involved in Morocco since 1871, when the loss of Alsace-Lorraine meant that the French were trading in Morocco for **minerals**. (See page 11.) The weakness of the country worried French politicians and in 1900 and 1901 they had made secret agreements with Italy that Morocco should come under French control. In April 1904, France and Britain agreed that France would have a **mandate** over Morocco and, in return, France would give up any remaining interests they had in Egypt, leaving that to Britain. However, at a time when Germany was looking to expand, no one had asked German politicians whether they would be comfortable with this arrangement.

GERMAN REACTION

The German emperor, Kaiser Wilhelm II, said publicly that all he was interested in was having equal economic rights in Morocco to those of other European countries.

German politicians went further than that. They were worried about the extension of French power in the Mediterranean Sea and North Africa. They assured Sultan Aziz of their support and encouraged him to resist France.

German politicians were looking for a 'place in the sun'. (See page 8.) While they were not particularly worried about the sultan, they wanted to show Britain and France that they, too, wanted colonies in Africa.

On 31 March 1905, Kaiser Wilhelm II landed at Tangier with the intention of showing a German interest in North Africa. He rode straight to the German embassy, where he spoke to all the officials who had gathered to meet him – French, German and Moroccan. He assured everyone of Germany's support for Sultan Aziz and for the independence of Morocco. He also stated that Germany knew best how to protect this independence, and he expected everyone to respect this. He left the building, and toured Tangier on a white horse, surrounded by officials and supporters. It was an impressive and dramatic display of support for the sultan.

EXTEND YOUR KNOWLEDGE

KAISER WILHELM'S VISIT TO TANGIER
Kaiser Wilhelm didn't really want to visit Tangier. He was on holiday, cruising in the Mediterranean with his family and having fun. He only agreed to go to Tangier after his Head of Security had personally visited the city and assured him that it was a safe place and he wouldn't be assassinated.

SOURCE A

A photograph of Kaiser Wilhelm II touring Tangier on 31 March 1905.

France and Britain reacted to the German position with shock. French press and politicians were angry. They had assumed that agreeing to French control over Morocco would be simple. Although the French government refused to risk war with Germany over the matter, all military leave was cancelled, just in case of further trouble.

The British government made it obvious that they would not tolerate Germany interfering in Morocco. They were afraid that Germany might be able to set up a naval base in one of Morocco's ports. This would threaten the British naval base at Gibraltar and could challenge British naval dominance. (See page 12.)

THE ALGECIRAS CONFERENCE 1906

A conference was held in Algeciras to settle the Moroccan situation. The conference lasted from 16 January to 7 April and was attended by 12 European countries and the USA. The only country to support Germany was Austria-Hungary. The final agreement between them was that France would have a controlling interest in Moroccan affairs, but every nation was free to trade with Morocco. Further, action in Morocco by any country had to be agreed by all the countries that had signed the final agreement.

The Algeciras Conference temporarily solved the problem. However, it only worsened tensions between the European powers. It showed that the Entente Cordiale was strong, as Britain had supported France against Germany. But it angered the German Kaiser, who felt he had been embarrassed and was determined not to back down in any future dispute. This led directly to the second Moroccan crisis.

THE SECOND MOROCCAN CRISIS, 1911–12

In March 1911, there was more trouble in Morocco. Rebel tribes once again rose up against the sultan and surrounded Fez. The sultan appealed to France for help, and France sent a small group of soldiers to Fez in May 1911. Spain did as well. Both governments claimed that they were doing this to protect French and Spanish people who were living in Fez.

GERMAN REACTION

German politicians, however, thought differently. They believed the French had deliberately encouraged a tribal **revolt** so that they could send troops to occupy Morocco. This went against the agreement reached at the Algeciras conference. On 1 July 1911, a German gunboat SMS *Panther* arrived in the Moroccan port of Agadir. Germany said it was there to protect the interests of German people living in Morocco.

The French reaction to the 'Agadir incident' was to send more troops into Morocco. British politicians tried to persuade France not to increase the tension by taking this action, but were unsuccessful. In the end, the British government agreed that there was no choice but to support France. Britain was increasingly concerned that Germany was planning to build a military base in the Mediterranean, and that this would be a direct threat to the British naval base in Gibraltar.

THE OUTCOME

Tensions between France, Britain and Germany were reaching breaking point when suddenly, and unexpectedly, Germany was hit by a financial crisis. German ministers could not deal with a domestic financial crisis and an international crisis at the same time. They ended their involvement in the international conflict over Morocco and signed the Treaty of Fez in November 1911. In it they agreed that France could take control of Morocco in exchange for granting Germany land in the Congo, which was a French colony in Africa.

The immediate crisis was over. There were, however, longer-term effects.
- British support for France further strengthened the Entente Cordiale of 1904.
- The division between the Entente powers and Germany increased.

Britain and France strengthened their friendship by making a naval agreement. The British Royal Navy would protect the northern coast of France from German attack, and the French fleet would protect British interests in the Mediterranean. In this way, the British navy could concentrate on the English Channel and the North Sea, in case it had to oppose the German High Seas Fleet. The French fleet would make sure France could keep communications open with French colonies in North Africa.

SOURCE B

A cartoon published in a British magazine on 2 August 1911.

SOLID.

GERMANY. "DONNERWETTER! IT'S ROCK. I THOUGHT IT WAS GOING TO BE PAPER."

ACTIVITY

1 Create a flow chart to show how events in Morocco during the years 1905–11 led to Britain and France coming closer together.

2 Look carefully at Source A. Imagine you are a German newspaper reporter. Use the information in this section to write the story that goes with the photograph. Remember you are writing for a German newspaper.

3 What is the message of the cartoon in Source B? Find the evidence in this section that backs up the message.

EXAM-STYLE QUESTION

A01

Describe **two** features of the second Moroccan crisis (1911–12).   **(6 marks)**

HINT

You need to identify two features of the second Moroccan crisis (1911–12). Don't just say what they were; add some detailed supporting information.

2.2 CRISIS IN THE BALKANS

LEARNING OBJECTIVES

- Understand the importance of the Balkans for fulfilling the ambitions of the European powers
- Understand the reasons why there was a Bosnian crisis in 1908–9
- Understand the impact of the Balkan Wars 1912–13 on Eastern Europe.

KEY TERM

annex to take control of a country or area next to your own

EXTEND YOUR KNOWLEDGE

THE SICK MAN OF EUROPE

Turkey was commonly known as the 'sick man of Europe'. This was a sign that the once great Ottoman Empire, that had ruled the Balkans and the eastern Mediterranean as far as the Caspian Sea, as well as Egypt and North Africa, was getting weaker.

1908 'Young Turk' revolution in Turkey
Austria **annexes** Bosnia-Herzegovina

1912 Greece, Bulgaria, Serbia and Montenegro form the **Balkan League**
First Balkan War between the Balkan League and Turkey

1913 Second Balkan War fought by Bulgaria against Serbia and Greece

The Balkans had once been part of the great Turkish Empire – the Ottoman Empire. As the power of the empire weakened, Turkey began to lose control over the Slav people living in the Balkans. They began rebelling against Turkish rule and demanding independence. By the early years of the 20th century, the Balkans was a very unstable part of Eastern Europe. Because of this, the powerful countries that bordered the Balkans began to take an interest in what was going on there. This could be their chance to increase their influence in the area by taking advantage of Turkey's weakness.

THE EUROPEAN POWERS: AIMS AND AMBITIONS IN THE BALKANS

The politicians in three of the major powers in Europe – Russia, Austria-Hungary and Germany – were all carefully watching the situation in the Balkans. They were waiting for a chance to extend their influence there, by taking land if they could.

AUSTRIA-HUNGARY

Austria-Hungary was an empire that contained many different nationalities, and the government was struggling to keep them united under the emperor. The Serbs made up one of these national groups, and just over the border from Austria-Hungary was Serbia. The last thing Austria-Hungary wanted was for Serbia to grow in power and influence, because that might encourage the Serbs in its empire to revolt in an attempt to join with Serbia. Austria-Hungary aimed to control Serbia along with any other troublesome Slav areas. A second aim was to gain more land with a coastline, and so more ports, on the Adriatic Sea.

RUSSIA

The Russians saw themselves as protectors of the Serbs. This was because the Russians, like the Serbs, were Slavs and shared similar languages and customs. Because of this, Russia would be likely to support Serbia in any dispute. The Russians were also keen to extend their power and influence in the Balkans because they hoped to have some sort of control over the Dardanelles, as this would give their Black Sea fleet guaranteed access to the Mediterranean.

GERMANY

Germany had a different sort of interest in the Balkans. Germany (see pages 10–11) was keen to build up its economic and industrial strength. There were extensive oil fields in Iraq, and Kaiser Wilhelm wanted to build a railway between Berlin and Baghdad. The railway would link the countries' capital cities and would be used to transport oil to Germany. It would have to pass through the Balkans.

▼ Figure 2.2 A map of the Balkans in 1914. The dates in brackets are the dates on which the different states won their independence from Turkey

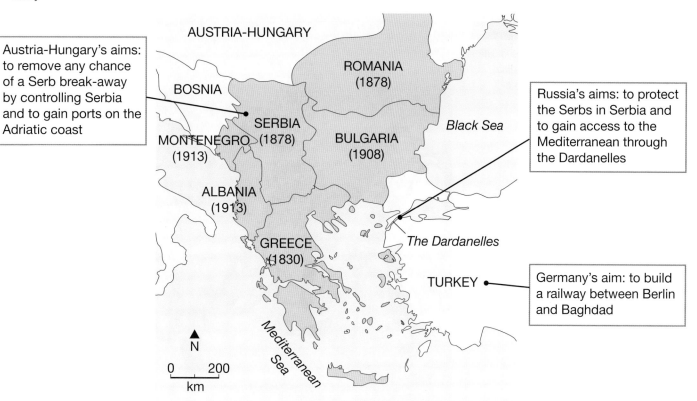

Austria-Hungary's aims: to remove any chance of a Serb break-away by controlling Serbia and to gain ports on the Adriatic coast

Russia's aims: to protect the Serbs in Serbia and to gain access to the Mediterranean through the Dardanelles

Germany's aim: to build a railway between Berlin and Baghdad

So three powerful countries in Europe were waiting and watching events in the Balkans. They all had something to gain and were just waiting for a chance to take it. The chance they were waiting for came in 1908.

THE BOSNIAN CRISIS, 1908–9

In 1908 a revolution shook Turkey. An organisation called the 'Young Turks' forced Turkey's ruler, Sultan Abdul Hamid, to restore Turkey's democratic **constitution**. It had been set up in 1876 but had only lasted 2 years. The chaos brought about by the revolution was the moment Austria-Hungary had been waiting for. While Turkey was busy with internal chaos, Austria annexed the provinces of Bosnia and Herzegovina and made them part of the Austro-Hungarian Empire. This had an immediate effect.

■ The king of Serbia claimed that the two provinces of Bosnia and Herzegovina should belong to Serbia. This was because most people living in the two provinces were Serbs. Serbia sent a formal protest to Austria-Hungary.

- Russia supported Serbia and protested to Austria-Hungary.
- Germany stepped into the row and made it obvious that it supported Austria-Hungary.

Neither Russia nor Serbia was prepared to risk war with Germany over this issue. Both countries decided to end their involvement in the dispute. The whole incident, however, encouraged Russia to increase the size of its army still further. It would not be caught out again.

Austria-Hungary wasn't the only country to take advantage of the revolution in Turkey. The ruler of Bulgaria, which was controlled by Turkey, crowned himself king and declared Bulgarian independence.

SOURCE C

A cartoon published in France in 1908. The artist is commenting on the annexation of Bosnia and Herzegovina by Austria-Hungary.

THE BALKAN WARS, 1912–13

The kings of Bulgaria, Greece, Montenegro and Serbia joined together in the Balkan League. The aim of the League was to force Turkey out of Europe.

THE FIRST BALKAN WAR (OCTOBER 1912–MAY 1913)

The First Balkan War was short and bloody; after 6 months it was all over. The Turkish troops could not compete with the combined armies of the Balkan states and after 50 days of actual fighting they surrendered. At the peace conference held in London, Turkey agreed to give up all their land in Europe. It was shared between the four countries of the Balkan League.

THE SECOND BALKAN WAR (JUNE 1913–AUGUST 1913)

King Ferdinand of Bulgaria was not satisfied with the way in which Turkey's European lands had been divided up between the Balkan League countries. A month after the peace conference in London, he ordered his troops to attack

Serbia and Greece. Serbian and Greek armies invaded Bulgaria, helped by Romania, which had been angry with Bulgaria for a long time. Turkish armies became involved too, hoping to gain some of the land they had lost. The fighting ended when Bulgaria asked for an **armistice**. Bulgaria had to give up some of the land it had gained as a result of the First Balkan War, most of which went to Serbia. Turkey regained some land, too.

As a result of the Balkan Wars:
- Serbia doubled in size and grew increasingly aggressive
- the Serbs in Bosnia-Herzegovina grew increasingly anxious and wanted to join Serbia
- Austria-Hungary grew increasingly worried about the possibility of revolt within its empire
- Austria-Hungary was determined to try to control Serbia
- Bulgaria was determined to take revenge on Serbia.

KEY TERM

armistice an agreement to stop fighting

BALKAN NATIONALISM

The Bosnian crisis strengthened the growth of nationalism in the Balkans. The Serbs in Austria-Hungary looked to Serbia for support and hoped to break away from Austria-Hungary and join Serbia. They were encouraged by the declaration of independence on the part of Bulgaria, where many Slav people lived. The Slavs in Bulgaria developed a sense of nationalism and loyalty to their own country as well as to the Slav peoples.

The Balkan Wars had seen this new sense of nationalism in action. A sense of Slav identity had brought Bulgaria, Greece, Montenegro and Serbia together into the Balkan League. It was nationalism that made King Ferdinand of Bulgaria demand more for Bulgaria than it had gained after the First Balkan War, and so started the second one. After the Second Balkan War, Serbia had grown in strength, size and influence. It became the focus of nationalism for Serbs throughout Eastern Europe. This made the situation even more dangerous than it had been before the Balkan Wars. Serbia was now a direct threat to the Austro-Hungarian Empire.

THE BLACK HAND

On 22 May 1911, ten young Serbian army officers met in Belgrade, the capital of Serbia, and formed a secret society. They called the secret society 'Unity or Death'. Its long-term aim was to unite all the Serbs outside Serbia who were ruled by Austria-Hungary or the Ottoman Empire. They planned to use terrorism to achieve their aim. The symbol of the society was a black hand, and so they were generally known as the 'Black Hand'. Before long, the society had over 2,500 members who were ready to die for their cause and promised to keep it secret. Their leader was Colonel Dragutin Dimitrievic, known as Apis. Its members were mainly army officers, like Apis, and some government officials. It conducted **propaganda campaigns**, organised armed bands and established a network of revolutionary units throughout Bosnia.

The first step, the society believed, was to get all the Serbs in Bosnia under Serbian rule. The situation was made more urgent by Austria's annexation of Bosnia. Apis made sure that all the troops guarding the border between Serbia and Bosnia were Black Hand members. This meant that terrorists could slip across the border and plant bombs, cut telegraph wires and carry out **assassinations** before returning to Serbia. Austria-Hungary, which had annexed Bosnia in 1908, was afraid the Serbs within their empire would revolt; they also suspected that Serbia was behind the individual acts of terrorism.

By 1914, the Balkans was a seething mixture of hatred, resentment, suspicion and aggression. It would take only a single event to cause the whole region to explode into a war that pulled in all the Great Powers.

EXAM-STYLE QUESTION

Describe **two** features of the Balkan Wars (1912–13).   **(6 marks)**

A01

> **HINT**
>
> You need to identify two features of the Balkan Wars. Don't just say what they were; add some detailed supporting information.

ACTIVITY

1 Imagine yourself as an adviser to Franz Joseph, the Emperor of Austria-Hungary. It is 1908 and Franz Joseph is considering annexing the provinces of Bosnia and Herzegovina. What advice do you give him, and why? (Remember it is 1908 and you won't know what happened as a result of the annexation.)

2 Look at the cartoon in Source C. What point is the cartoonist making? Do you think the cartoonist is on the side of Austria-Hungary or Bosnia-Herzegovina? Give your reasons.

3 In 1905, Serbia was a small and unimportant Balkan country. By 1914, Serbia had become one of the most powerful and dangerous Balkan states. Draw a flow chart showing how this happened.

4 Work with a partner.

  a You have both been recruited into the Black Hand secret society. Draw up a plan of action that will lead to your long-term objective – the creation of a Slav state. Remember that really big objectives, like this one, are achieved by a series of small steps.

  b Compare your ideas with others in your class. Which ideas are the most likely to be successful?

2.3 MURDER AT SARAJEVO

LEARNING OBJECTIVES

- Understand the significance of the visit of Archduke Franz Ferdinand to Sarajevo
- Understand the events in Sarajevo on 28 June 1914 that led to the assassination of Archduke Franz Ferdinand and his wife
- Understand why the murder of Archduke Franz Ferdinand led to the First World War.

The event that **triggered** an all-out war came in 28 June 1914 in Sarajevo, the capital city of Bosnia. It was here that members of the Black Hand (see page 27) killed the **heir to the throne** of Austria-Hungary. The death of Archduke Franz Ferdinand was the event that caused Balkan tensions to explode and led to the First World War in August 1914.

SARAJEVO 1914: THE SIGNIFICANCE OF FRANZ FERDINAND'S VISIT

EXTEND YOUR KNOWLEDGE

FRANZ FERDINAND AND SOPHIE CHOTEK

Archduke Franz Ferdinand married the Countess Sophie Chotek on 28 June 1900. The Austro-Hungarian emperor, Franz Joseph, had opposed the marriage. This was because a countess was not high enough in social importance for an archduke to marry. No children of the marriage were allowed to inherit the throne, and Sophie was not permitted to be by his side on any state occasion. He was visiting Sarajevo as head of the army, so it was not an official state visit and Sophie was allowed to accompany him.

Tension in the Balkans was rising and the activities of the Black Hand worried the Austro-Hungarian government. Government advisers were suggesting that a quick war with Serbia would end any Slav rebellion before it even started. It was time, politicians and the military believed, for a show of strength.

The Austro-Hungarian government decided that Archduke Franz Ferdinand, the heir to the Austro-Hungarian Empire, would make an official visit to Bosnia in June 1914. As head of the army, he would first watch army exercises and then go to the capital, Sarajevo, where city officials would welcome him and his wife. The date chosen was 28 June, the national day of the Serbian people. The visit was given a lot of pre-publicity. This publicity was just what the Black Hand needed. Members now knew exactly where Franz Ferdinand was going to be, and when. To assassinate the heir to the Austro-Hungarian throne would strike a terrible blow at the empire they hated.

EXTRACT A

From a modern history book.

Franz Ferdinand was a brutal and obstinate man, impatient with opposition, unsuited to a democratic age. He had one redeeming feature: he loved his wife. It annoyed him that she could never share his splendours. There was one loophole. His wife could enjoy the recognition of his rank when he was acting in a military capacity. Hence, he decided, in 1914, to inspect the army in Bosnia. There, at its capital Sarajevo, the archduke and his wife could ride in an open carriage, side by side on 28 June – their wedding anniversary. Thus, for love, did the Archduke go to his death.

SARAJEVO: THE ASSASSINATION

28 June 1914 was a warm and sunny day when Archduke Franz Ferdinand and his wife Sophie arrived in Sarajevo. The troop inspection had gone well, and they were now looking forward to their visit to the city. They arrived there by train, and waiting for them was a large open-topped car that was to be part of a motorcade driving them to the town hall. The streets were lined by cheering crowds. However, hiding among the cheering crowds were members of the Black Hand secret society, who were planning murder. At first, their plan did not go well. One would-be assassin couldn't get his revolver out of his jacket in time; another felt sorry for Sophie and went home, and a third threw a bomb but it missed its target. Franz Ferdinand was furious. His day out with his wife had been ruined. When the royal car reached the town hall, he shouted angrily at the mayor and cancelled the visit. On the way back to the station, the chauffeur took a wrong turn. He stopped the car, getting ready to reverse. It was then that Gavrilo Princip, one of the would-be assassins, saw what was happening. Reacting quickly, he pulled out his revolver and fired two shots. One bullet hit Franz Ferdinand in the throat; the other hit Sophie in the stomach. With blood pouring from their wounds, they were driven off at high speed to the Bosnian governor's house, where they could receive medical attention. By midnight, Archduke Franz Ferdinand and his wife Sophie were dead.

Princip tried to commit suicide by swallowing the poison cyanide, but it failed to work. Then he tried to shoot himself, but the police caught and arrested him before he could do that. At his trial, he was sentenced to 20 years in prison, because at 19 years of age at the time of the assassination, he was too young to hang.

A painting of the assassination of Archduke Franz Ferdinand on 28 June 1914. The picture was published in a French magazine the following month.

EXTEND YOUR KNOWLEDGE

NEDELJKO CABRINOVIC

Nedeljko was one of the would-be assassins in Sarajevo on 28 June 1914. He threw the bomb that missed its target, the car carrying the Archduke and his wife. When Cabrinovic saw what had happened, he took a cyanide pill, intending to commit suicide. However, the pill was out-of-date and it only made him sick. He next tried to drown himself by jumping into a river, but it was only 10 cm deep. The police arrested him.

Princip

I knew it was the Archduke, but there was a lady with him, so I wasn't sure whether to shoot. But it was easy to shoot because the car was going slowly. So I fired at the Archduke. I think I fired twice, perhaps more, but I am not sure because I was so excited. I don't know if I hit anyone because the crowd started attacking me.

I was told to watch the crowd, not the car. I heard a gunshot, then a second one. I charged through the crowd and grabbed the assassin by the arm. Then someone punched me hard in the stomach.

Detective

Today we will investigate your crime of murder. You shot from the closest distance with a Browning pistol at the Archduke and his wife, with the intention to kill them. You hit them both, which caused their deaths a short time afterwards.

Judge

▲ **Figure 2.3** What they said about the assassination

ACTIVITY

1 Write a report to Apis, the leader of the Black Hand, about the actions of Black Hand members in Sarajevo on 28 June 1914. Clearly members had been successful in that Franz Ferdinand had been assassinated, but was this more by luck or careful planning? Remember to cover the negatives as well as the positives in your report.

2 The artist who painted Source D was not there at the time. Match the detail in the painting with the evidence about what happened on 28 June. Would a photograph have given us a clearer idea about the shooting?

3 Look at Figure 2.3.
 a List the points about which Princip is certain, and list the points about which he is uncertain. Why do you think he can't be sure about what he had done?
 b Now look at what the detective and the judge say. How helpful are they in clearing up the uncertainties in Princip's account?

4 Do you think events in Sarajevo would have ended in the way they did if it had been pouring with rain? Discuss this in class.

THE COUNTDOWN TO WAR IN 1914: THE JULY DAYS

5 July Germany agrees to support Austria-Hungary

25 July Serbia agrees to all demands except one

28 July Austria-Hungary declares war on Serbia Serbia asks Russia for help

31 July Germany warns France not to intervene

2 August Germany asks Belgium to let German troops through into France; Belgium refuses

4 August Britain declares war on Germany

28 June Assassination of Archduke Franz Ferdinand

23 July Austria-Hungary sends demands to Serbia

26 July Russia promises to help Serbia

29 July Germany warns Russia not to intervene Russia mobilises

1 August Germany declares war on Russia France mobilises

3 August Germany declares war on France German troops enter Belgium

The period between the murder of Franz Ferdinand and the start of the First World War is known as the 'July days'. As the timeline shows, a lot happened in July 1914. But just how did an assassination in the Balkans end with Europe at war?

A BALKAN PROBLEM

The two previous Balkan Wars had not developed into a massive European, or even a world, war. At first, it looked very much as though the assassination would cause a third Balkan war. Franz Joseph was convinced that the Serbian government had supported the Black Hand in the assassination. The events in Sarajevo gave Austria-Hungary the opportunity to hit back at Serbia. The First and Second Balkan Wars had stayed local and had not led to a war between the Triple Entente and Triple Alliance countries. Care had to be taken not to involve them in any action Austria-Hungary took against Serbia. Austria-Hungary turned to its ally, Germany, for support. On 5 July Wilhelm II and his chancellor, Bethmann-Holwegg, told the Austrians to take a strong line with Serbia and promised German support if Russia threatened to support Serbia.

Austria-Hungary looked for proof that Serbia had been involved in the Sarajevo assassination, but could find none. Nevertheless, on 23 July they sent a list of demands to Serbia. These demands included a **suppression** of anti-Austrian publications and organisations, the arrest of Serbian officials involved in the plot to assassinate the Archduke Franz Ferdinand, and the involvement of Serbia in an enquiry into the assassination. Serbia agreed to all the demands, except one. This was that Austria-Hungary would send officials into Serbia to make sure that all traces of the Black Hand organisation had been wiped out. Serbia could not agree to this because it would mean an end to Serbia's independence.

Austria-Hungary broke off diplomatic relations with Serbia and on 28 July declared war; Austro-Hungarian cannons in Bosnia began shelling Belgrade.

For the third time in 3 years, war had broken out in the Balkans. What happened to turn it into a world war?

COUNTDOWN TO A WORLD WAR, 1914

29 July

Russia supported the Serbs as being part of the huge Slav group of people. Because of this, when Serbia asked for help, Russia could not allow Serbia to be embarrassed. Added to this, if Germany and Austria-Hungary dominated the Balkans, Russia's access to the Mediterranean would be controlled by potential enemies. Russia could not allow this to happen. Tsar Nicholas of Russia ordered the Russian army to mobilise.

30 July – 1 August

The next day, 30 July 1914, the German Kaiser, Wilhelm II, sent an ultimatum to Tsar Nicholas, ordering him to stop mobilising his army. Nicholas refused to accept the ultimatum and so Germany declared war on Russia. The German army was mobilised. As France was an ally of Russia, the French government ordered the mobilisation of its army.

2 August

Germany began to put the Schlieffen Plan (see page 14) into operation. Army trains started leaving Cologne station in Germany at the rate of one every three minutes, heading for the German border with Belgium.

3 August

The position of Britain was complicated. By the terms of the 1904 Entente Cordiale (see page 5), it did not have to join in a war in support of France. However, many politicians were afraid that German success against France would result in a German-dominated Europe. This would threaten British trade and possibly the independence of Britain itself.

In 1839, Great Britain had given Belgium a guarantee of protection against any attack by another country. This was the Treaty of London, and it had been signed by Britain, France, Russia, Austria and Prussia. (By 1914, Prussia was an important part of Germany.) A German invasion of Belgium would break that treaty. Now that Germany was preparing to invade Belgium, the British government decided to honour the guarantee made 75 years earlier. The Treaty of London was signed long before any of the tensions that led to the First World War had even been thought of, but for many in the British government, it gave them just the acceptable excuse they needed to go to war. So a **telegram** was sent to the German Kaiser, ordering him to call his army back to within the borders of Germany. The German government was given until midnight on 4 August to reply.

4 August

German troops moved quickly into Belgium. Only a small Belgian army opposed them, but the Belgians did manage to blow up the railway lines leading to their border with France. This cut down the speed of the German advance towards France because it slowed down the movement of German supplies and additional soldiers.

By midnight, the British government had not received a reply to its telegram to the Kaiser, and so Britain was at war with Germany.

BRAVO, BELGIUM!

5 August
The Triple Alliance and the Triple Entente were at war with each other.

The involvement of Great Britain, with its worldwide empire, turned what could have been a European war into a world war.

THE ROLE OF THE GREAT POWERS IN THE START OF THE WAR

Tension between the Great Powers in Europe had existed since the start of 20th century, so why did war break out in 1914 when it had been avoided in earlier years? The answer to this question is that by 1914 the rivalries between the powers had become so strong that it just took one event to trigger a war. The assassination of the Austrian Archduke in Sarajevo was that event. It was a very serious event, but it was not really a reason for the powers to become involved in 4 years of terrible fighting. It was the political, economic, colonial and military rivalries between the powers that caused the war.

Britain feared that Germany was trying to threaten its economic and colonial supremacy and build a navy bigger than Britain's. France also felt that its colonies were threatened and wanted Alsace-Lorraine back from Germany. The Germans wanted their 'place in the sun' and were building a powerful navy to help win it. They knew that France would want a war of revenge following Germany's victory in the Franco-Prussian war, so they allied with Austria-Hungary to make themselves stronger. The Austrians were rivals with Russia in the Balkans and wanted to keep the growing movement for Slavic independence under control. Russia was keen to help the Slavs! By the time of the assassination it looked like these rivalries could only be resolved by war. So when Austria-Hungary threatened Serbia, instead of meeting to resolve the problem, the Great Powers lined up for war.

ACTIVITY

1 Work with a partner.
   a On a sheet of paper draw two columns. Head one column 'Reasons why Germany went to war in 1914' and head the other 'Reasons why Great Britain went to war in 1914'. List as many reasons as you can. (Hint: you may want to look back at Chapter 1.)
   b Colour-code those reasons, with the long-term reasons in one colour and the short-term reasons (those that only happened in 1914) in another colour.
   c Share your ideas with the rest of your class. Come up with a list of long-term and short-term causes with which you all agree.
2 Working in a small group, use the information your class has put together in answer to (c) to draw a spider diagram showing the connections between the long-term and the short-term causes. Use the diagram to write a paragraph of not more than 150 words to explain why war broke out in 1914.
3 Now look at the cartoon in Source E. What point is the cartoonist making? How would a cartoon showing Belgium and Germany have been different if a German cartoonist had drawn it? What different point would he or she have tried to make?

RECAP

RECALL QUIZ

1   Name the Moroccan city visited by Wilhelm II in 1905.
2   In what year was the Algeciras Conference?
3   Where did Kaiser Wilhelm II send a gunboat in 1911?
4   Between which cities did Kaiser Wilhelm II want to build a railway?
5   When did Austria-Hungary annex Bosnia-Herzegovina?
6   Which four countries made up the Balkan League?
7   Name the secret society formed in Serbia in May 1911.
8   Which town in Bosnia did Archduke Franz Ferdinand and his wife visit in June 1914?
9   When did Russia mobilise?
10 What happened on 4 August 1914?

CHECKPOINT

STRENGTHEN

S1 Why did Germany become involved in Morocco?
S2 Give two reasons why the growth of Serbia threatened the stability of Europe.
S3 Why did Britain declare war on Germany in 1914? Give two reasons.

CHALLENGE

C1 Explain how the Moroccan situation (1905–11) strengthened relationships between Britain and France.
C2 How important was Balkan nationalism in creating tension in Europe between October 1912 and July 1914?
C3 To what extent was Germany to blame for starting the First World War?

SUMMARY

- Germany wanted colonies in Africa and this challenged France and Britain.
- The Algeciras Conference (1906) gave France a controlling influence in Moroccan affairs. This angered Germany.
- The Treaty of Fez (1911) gave France control over Morocco and gave Germany control over part of the Congo.
- The Triple Entente countries became increasingly suspicious about Germany's ambitions.
- In 1908, Austria-Hungary annexed the provinces of Bosnia-Herzegovina. Most people living there were Serbs.
- The Balkan Wars (1912–13) led to Serbia doubling in size. Austria-Hungary was concerned its Serbs would revolt against Austrian rule.
- A Serbian secret society assassinated Archduke Franz Ferdinand in June 1914.
- Austria-Hungary declared war on Serbia in July 1914. Germany supported Austria-Hungary and Russia supported Serbia.
- By 4 August 1914, the two alliances were at war with each other.

3. THE SCHLIEFFEN PLAN AND DEADLOCK ON THE WESTERN FRONT

LEARNING OBJECTIVES

- Understand the impact of the failure of the Schlieffen Plan
- Understand the life and fighting in the trenches
- Understand the significance of key battles, such as the Somme and Passchendaele.

Once war was declared between the countries of the Triple Entente and the countries of the Triple Alliance, war plans swung into action. In some countries it was confidently believed that the war would be over by Christmas, and young men in Britain and France, Germany and Austria-Hungary volunteered for the army, anxious not to be left out. The war began with a rapid German advance through Belgium and France. That advance, however, quickly stopped and the armies 'dug in'. By December 1914, a line of trenches stretched from the English Channel to Switzerland in an area known as the 'Western Front'. Here, hundreds of thousands of lives were lost as men struggled to gain, avoid losing and regain sometimes less than a kilometre of the countryside they had destroyed. The use of machine guns, tanks, gas and even aeroplanes did little to break the deadlock. It was stalemate. Neither side had the manpower, the tactics or the equipment to defeat the other. By the end of 1917, there was deadlock on the Western Front and neither side seemed able to break it.

3.1 THE SCHLIEFFEN PLAN FAILS

LEARNING OBJECTIVES

☐ Understand the impact of the failure of the Schlieffen Plan

☐ Understand why there was a race for the sea

☐ Understand the significance of the ending of the war of movement.

Immediately after war was declared, the Great Powers began to put their war plans into operation. (Look again at page 14 to remind yourself what these were.) Thousands of men were on the move.

■ The British sent four **infantry** divisions and one **cavalry** division to France. This was made up of 80,000 men and 30,000 horses, and was called the British Expeditionary Force (BEF). The whole army landed at French ports and headed east, to the border between France and Belgium.

■ Over 1 million French soldiers gathered on the German border ready to invade Alsace-Lorraine.

■ Facing the British and French were three enormous German armies that were pushing through Belgium. One was heading straight for the BEF, and the other two towards the French forces.

THE FAILURE OF THE SCHLIEFFEN PLAN

The success of the German Schlieffen Plan (see page 14) depended on speed. France was to be invaded by a high-speed German advance through Belgium so that, once Paris was taken, France would surrender. Germany could then turn to fight Russia, a country that would be slow to mobilise. That was the theory. It didn't quite work out that way. The German advance through Belgium was slower than expected and the BEF helped delay the advance at the battle of Mons in August. Russia mobilised its forces more quickly than expected and the Germans had to withdraw troops from the advance to fight the Russians. The delay meant that the Germans had to change their plans so that their troops avoided Paris. In September they met French and British troops at the battle of the Marne. After a week of fighting, the German advance was stopped and their forces retreated 60 km to set up defensive positions along the River Aisne.

▼ **Figure 3.1** Why did the Schlieffen Plan fail?

1. The battle of Mons (23–24 August 1914)
The BEF slowed the German advance for 48 hours before British troops were forced to retreat.

2. Collapse of Plan 17
French armies failed to re-capture Alsace and Lorraine, but slowed the German advance into France by 2 weeks.

Why did the Schlieffen Plan fail?

3. Russian mobilisation
Russia mobilised quickly and on 19 August invaded eastern Germany. German troops had to be moved from the Western Front to defend Germany's eastern borders.

4. The battle of the Marne (5–11 September 1914)
The German army, not strong enough to take Paris, swung east towards the River Marne. There they clashed with the French forces retreating from Alsace and Lorraine and, with the BEF, were beaten back to the River Aisne.

EXTEND YOUR KNOWLEDGE

THE BATTLE OF THE MARNE
The battle of the Marne was fought so close to Paris that the French ferried men to the battlefront in taxis. A fleet of 250 taxis shuttled back and forward throughout the week, taking fresh men to fight the exhausted Germans.

KEY TERM

stalemate a situation in which neither side can get an advantage

▶ **Figure 3.2** The Western Front in December 1914

The Schlieffen Plan had failed. Both sides dug trenches to defend themselves and to stop the other side advancing. By December 1914, lines of trenches stretched along the Western Front from the English Channel to Switzerland. For the next 4 years two enormous armies faced each other across these lines of trenches. Neither side could advance by more than a few kilometres. Extremely violent battles would be fought to gain only a few hundred metres of land. There was **stalemate** on the Western Front; neither side could move. It looked as though the outcome of the war would be decided by whichever side could work out how to break through the other side's line of trenches.

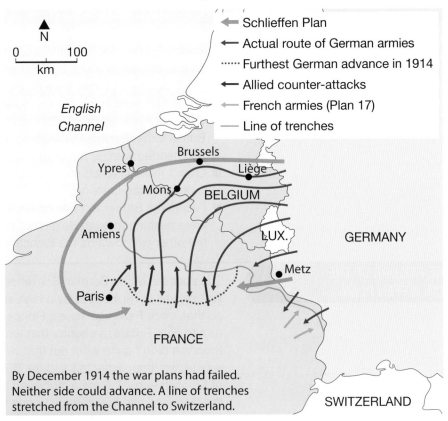

By December 1914 the war plans had failed. Neither side could advance. A line of trenches stretched from the Channel to Switzerland.

ACTIVITY

1 Look back at the reasons why the Schlieffen Plan failed. (See Figure 3.1.) Which reason, in your judgement, was the most important in bringing about failure? Write three or four sentences to explain why. Compare your decision with those of others in your class, and see if you can reach agreement about which was the most important.

2 It is August 1914. Work in three groups. One group must take on the role of adviser to the German generals, one group as adviser to the French and one group as adviser to the British generals. Each group must work out a strategy for success. You will all need to bear in mind your answer to question 1, and try to avoid that. Choose a spokesperson for each group and compare your strategies. What would be the likely outcome of each?

3 Most people thought that the war would be 'over by Christmas'. Why were they wrong? Write a paragraph in explanation.

4 After the battle of the Marne, General von Moltke said to the German Kaiser, 'Sir, we have lost the war.' Why do you think he was so sure at such an early stage as September 1914?

3.2 LIVING IN THE TRENCHES

LEARNING OBJECTIVES

- Understand how the trench systems supported the troops
- Understand conditions in the trenches
- Understand the ways in which soldiers adapted to life in the trenches.

TRENCH SYSTEMS

In the winter of 1914, both sides dug in along the Western Front with complicated systems of trenches. British and French trenches were usually just over 2 m deep and 1.8 m wide. German trenches were often deeper. The trench systems had front-line trenches, where the fighting was done. Behind them was a series of communication, reserve and support trenches. These were where the kitchens and lavatories were placed, as well as field hospitals and the battalion headquarters.

The top of the front-line trenches was protected by sandbags that absorbed enemy bullets. In front of the sandbags was **barbed wire** to trap enemy soldiers who made it across **no-man's-land**, the area between German and Allied front lines. In no-man's-land were 'small posts' that were used for listening to the enemy's movements and were sometimes occupied at night in the hope of gaining an advantage next day. Rest for the front-line soldier came from short moments of sleep in the **dug-outs**. The whole trench system was dug in a Z pattern, making it impossible for the enemy to fire straight down the line of trenches if they were captured.

DEADLOCK ON THE WESTERN FRONT

KEY TERM

deadlock a situation in which no progress can be made. Sometimes historians also refer to 'stalemate' on the Western Front

The trenches were a reaction to the **deadlock** in the fighting. Why was there deadlock?

- The failure of the German Schlieffen Plan: once the German advance was stopped in 1914, a series of trenches was dug from the sea to the Swiss mountains. The Germans generally 'dug in' at places that were difficult to attack, and the Allies had great difficulty breaking through.
- The strength of defences: the trench systems were very difficult to attack, not only because of the barbed wire and sandbags, but even more because of the machine guns. Troops crossing no-man's-land were likely to be killed before the enemy trenches were reached.
- Ineffective weapons: the attacking weapons were not as effective as the machine gun was in defence. Attackers had some success with artillery, and poison gas worked in places. But the real keys to success in trench warfare were **tanks** and planes, and these were not sufficiently developed by 1914 to make a significant difference.
- The mud: the geography of the area also made advances difficult. Flanders was a particularly wet area and constant shelling and troop movement just churned up the area so that it was incredibly hard to cross – even if the enemy wasn't firing at you at the time!
- Lack of new **tactics**: many of the generals had been trained in the 'old' type of warfare which involved cavalry charges and hand-to-hand fighting. They had not got the experience or skills to work out how war could be fought in the unusual circumstances of trench warfare.

▶ **Figure 3.3** Plan of a trench system and cross-section of a trench

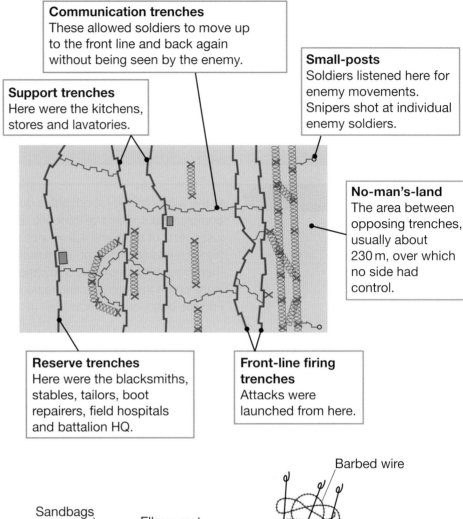

Communication trenches
These allowed soldiers to move up to the front line and back again without being seen by the enemy.

Support trenches
Here were the kitchens, stores and lavatories.

Small-posts
Soldiers listened here for enemy movements. Snipers shot at individual enemy soldiers.

No-man's-land
The area between opposing trenches, usually about 230 m, over which no side had control.

Reserve trenches
Here were the blacksmiths, stables, tailors, boot repairers, field hospitals and battalion HQ.

Front-line firing trenches
Attacks were launched from here.

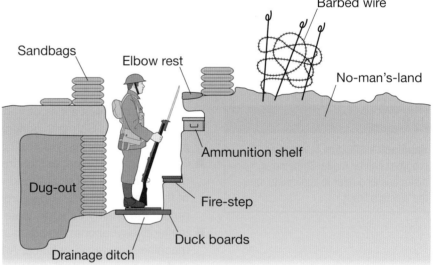

Barbed wire

Sandbags

Elbow rest

No-man's-land

Ammunition shelf

Dug-out

Fire-step

Duck boards

Drainage ditch

LIFE IN THE TRENCHES

Soldiers on the Western Front did not spend all their time in the trenches. The normal schedule in the British trenches was that men spent 4 days in the front-line trenches, 4 days in the support trenches, 8 days in reserve trenches and 14 days resting. If a battle was taking place, however, everyone had to stay in the front line and fight.

Although the trenches were a terrifying place during battle, most of the time very little was happening. So boredom was one of the most difficult aspects of day-time trench life for many soldiers. The day often involved routine work such as sentry duty, trench repair or bringing supplies from reserves trenches. In the front-line trenches, night was a time of silence and fear. Selected groups of men were sent on night patrol, crawling through the mud, filth, shell-holes and decaying bodies of no-man's-land to spot enemy activity. Sometimes there was a night attack on enemy trenches, taking prisoners and gaining information about what the other side was planning.

SOURCE A

A working party of British soldiers on the Somme, July 1916.

KEY TERMS

censor to remove any information that was not acceptable to the authorities

Flanders an area of northern France and Belgium; the principal town was Ypres

SOURCE B

British field postcard.

NOTHING is to be written on this side **except the date and signature of the sender. Sentences not required may be erased. If anything else is added the post card will be destroyed.**

I am quite well.

I have been admitted into hospital
{ *sick* } *and am going on well.*
{ *wounded* } *and hope to be discharged soon.*

I am being sent down to the base.

I have received your { *letter dated_____*
{ *telegram „ _____*
{ *parcel „ _____*

Letter follows at first opportunity.

I have received no letter from you
{ *lately.*
{ *for a long time.*

Signature)
only. }

Date_____

[Postage must be prepaid on any letter or post card addressed to the sender of this card.]

(25090) W t.W54,7-215* 1,000m. 2;15 M.R.Co.,Ltd.

Soldiers never knew when they would be able to get home, and often it was over a year before they saw their family and friends again. Soldiers in the front line were only allowed to send field postcards (see Source B), but those further away from the fighting could write letters home. These letters were usually **censored** by the authorities to ensure that nothing was accidentally given away that would help the enemy. Families and organisations, like the British Red Cross and the German Deutsches Rotes Kreuz, sent parcels of 'luxuries' to the troops – razor blades and soap, cigarettes, cake and chocolate, hand-knitted socks and gloves.

EXTEND YOUR KNOWLEDGE

THE WIPERS TIMES
During a pause in the fighting around the French town of Ypres, a group of British soldiers found an old printing press. They got it working and produced a magazine called the 'Wipers Times'. ('Wipers' was the way most British soldiers pronounced 'Ypres'.) The magazine joked about British officers through cartoons, advertisements, letters and announcements, as well as articles that made fun of their living conditions and battle plans. It was very popular.

DIRT AND DISEASE
In order to fight efficiently, men must be kept fit and well. Trenches were not healthy places: troops had to face cold, mud and the side effects of sleeping rough. Dominating all efforts at remaining healthy was mud. The ground in **Flanders** easily turned into a sea of mud. Men and horses drowned in it.

A photograph of trench foot.

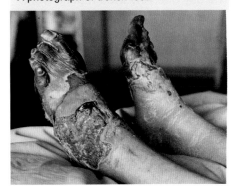

LATRINES (LAVATORIES)

The regulation latrines were pits 1.5 m deep dug in small trenches at the back of the main ones. A bucket was put in each pit. When it was full, a soldier had to empty the contents. This was a job often used as a punishment. Many soldiers hated using them and so used a spare tin or helmet instead, and threw the contents into no-man's-land. For paper, they used grass or the tail of a shirt.

DISEASE

Many soldiers caught colds, 'flu, bronchitis and trench fever, which was spread by lice. Ulcers, boils and skin diseases were common because soldiers scratched lice bites with dirty fingers. The hospital admission lists for 1917 show that thousands of soldiers had dysentery, frostbite, nephritis (a kidney disease), tuberculosis and pneumonia.

gangrenous a condition in which the flesh decays because blood has stopped flowing there as a result of illness or injury

sniper someone who shoots at people from a hidden position

Mud quickly coated boots, socks and trousers, which could not be changed for at least a week. 'Trench foot' was a common problem. Men standing for hours in very wet trenches without being able to change socks and boots ended up with feet that went numb and turned red and blue. If not treated, trench foot could turn **gangrenous**, and amputation was then the only treatment. During the winter of 1914–15, over 20,000 men in the British army were treated for trench foot.

It was often difficult to get food up to the front line because everything had to be carried along the communication trenches. The standard food was bully beef, hard biscuits, bread, margarine and jam, with occasional cheese and bacon. Tea was drunk in large quantities and sweetened with **condensed milk**. It was only when men went back down the line that they were able to get regular hot meals from the army field kitchens.

It was almost impossible to keep clean in the trenches. Most soldiers were infected with body **lice** that lived by sucking their blood. Lice were found in warm places on the soldiers' bodies and in the seams of their clothes. It was common for over 100 lice to be found crawling around on a single soldier. The only way to kill a **louse** was by squashing it or by burning it with a candle or lighted cigarette. Second only to soldiers' hatred of lice was their hatred of rats. The trenches swarmed with them, growing fat on left-over food and rotting bodies in no-man's-land. Flies, too, were a problem as they carried disease. The horses on the Western Front produced about 40 tons of manure every day, and flies multiplied in the manure.

CASUALTIES

Always, hanging over everyone, was the threat of sudden death, either from a **sniper**'s bullet or a planned attack, when soldiers would be expected to go 'over the top' of their trenches and attack the enemy on the other side of no-man's-land. Men lived with the sight, sound and smell of dead, dying and wounded soldiers. Thousands were killed or wounded in every battle, either by shelling or by machine-gun fire. Between battles, hundreds more were killed or wounded in night raids on enemy trenches and by snipers.

A soldier on the Western Front remembers seeing his first dead soldier.

Never before had I seen a man who had just been killed. A glance was enough. His face and body were terribly gashed as though some terrific force had pressed him down, and blood flowed from a dozen fearful wounds. The smell of blood mixed with the fumes of the shell filled me with nausea. Only a great effort saved my limbs from giving way beneath me. I could see from the sick grey faces of the men that these feelings were generally shared. A voice seemed to whisper, 'Why shouldn't you be next?'

During a battle, most **casualties** happened in no-man's-land and at night **stretcher** parties searched for the wounded who were too badly hurt to get back to their trenches on their own. When it was dark, all the wounded were taken back, through the communication trenches, to where regimental medical officers assessed who needed further medical help and who could be given **first aid** and sent back to fight. Soldiers who were seriously wounded were

SHELL-SHOCK

By the end of the First World War, the British army had dealt with over 80,000 cases of shell-shock. At first, medical officers believed that shell-shock was the result of a physical injury to a soldier's nerves by, for example, being buried alive. Treatment was massage, rest, good food and, if these failed, electric shock treatment. Gradually, medical opinion shifted to believing that shell-shock was a psychological condition. Treatment then was counselling, rest and, sometimes, hypnosis. At all times, the focus was on getting the soldiers fit to go back to the front. They were encouraged to behave like men and face up to war. Few shell-shock sufferers received sympathy from their family and friends, who often felt ashamed of them because they thought they were behaving like cowards.

KEY TERM

desert when a soldier leaves the army, navy or air force without permission

▶ The problems and dangers of trench life

sent to Casualty Clearing Stations (CCS) situated several kilometres behind the trenches. The injured who were too badly hurt to move were operated on at the CCS; others were taken, sometimes by train, to base hospitals. Depending on the treatment they needed, some of the injured stayed at base hospitals until they recovered; others were sent home to hospitals and nursing homes. Many died from their wounds or from infection. In the dirt and filth of battle, wounds quickly became infected. Antibiotics were not developed until the 1930s, and so during the First World War the only treatment was to keep the wound as clean as possible.

The fear of death and the death of friends were two of the worst things a soldier had to live with. Many just could not cope with the horrors they saw and heard. Their hands shook and their eyes twitched. Some could not hear or speak; others screamed or moaned, rocking backwards and forwards and shivering violently whenever guns fired. Some replayed in their minds, again and again, the sight and sound of the men they had killed: the horror, for example, of pulling a bayonet out of the body of a dying enemy soldier. This condition was called shell-shock. At first, sufferers were seen as cowards, but gradually doctors accepted that this was a psychological condition. Men with shell-shock were treated well away from the front. Some never recovered.

Some men were not able to cope with the horrors of war and **deserted**. They did this for many reasons: fear, shell-shock, problems at home or just complete exhaustion. If deserters were caught, they were put to death by firing squad. During the war, 346 British soldiers were shot for desertion.

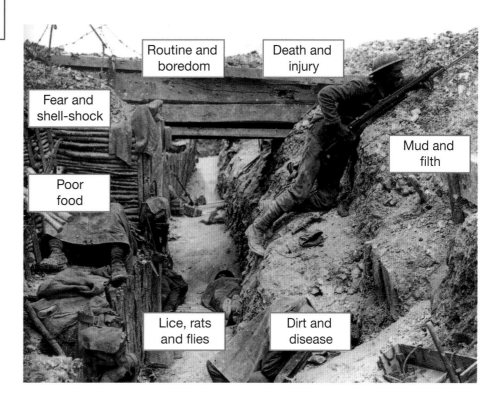

Routine and boredom

Death and injury

Fear and shell-shock

Mud and filth

Poor food

Lice, rats and flies

Dirt and disease

ACTIVITY

1 Look at the photo 'The problems and dangers of trench life'. Make a list of the problems and dangers of trench life, with the worst one at the top of the list. Explain why you put that one at the top.

2 Work in pairs. One of you is a cheerful soldier and the other complains a lot. Decide which soldier would have said each of these sentences: 'I like working hard, getting ready to fight the enemy'; 'The rats are eating our food'; 'Borrow my cigarette to burn the lice in your underpants'; 'I'm proud to be fighting for my country'; 'I'm terrified we'll be told to go over the top'; and 'I think I'm getting trench foot'. Now add some sentences of your own using the information in this section. Act out your dialogue to the class.

3 You are in the front line but want to get a message home. All you can use is the British field postcard. (See Source B.) How will you get a different, more personal, message past the censors? You could, for example, cross out some of the letters in the official words to make different ones. Many front-line soldiers did this.

3.3 NEW WEAPONS AND METHODS

LEARNING OBJECTIVES

- Understand the new types of weapons introduced
- Understand the strengths and weaknesses of the new weapons
- Understand the new fighting methods used.

KEY TERM

attrition the process of gradually destroying or weakening your enemy by attacking them continuously

In 1914, the generals on both sides had confidently believed that the war would be fought by quick-moving armies. By the start of 1915, however, there were millions of men dug into strong positions in trenches, facing equally strong positions on the other side of no-man's-land. Many thought that new technology could break the stalemate. Others disagreed, and thought that only by **attrition** would the war be won. The enemy had to be weakened by continual attacks that would eventually cause them to surrender. This approach to war depended on manpower; the side with the most men to throw into the **combat** would win. It would also lead to huge numbers of dead and wounded.

AIRCRAFT

In 1914, no one knew whether or not aircraft would play an important part in the war. The first plane had flown only 11 years earlier, and the Great Powers had only a few hundred planes each. These were made of wood and thick cloth, held together with piano wire. **Cockpits** were open and pilots had to wear layers of warm clothes, thick gloves, leather helmets and **goggles** to stop them from freezing to death in the air. There were few instruments. Engines were unreliable and there were no parachutes. Courage was needed just to fly a plane, let alone fight in one.

The British Royal Flying Corps and the Imperial German Flying Corps used planes and observation balloons as the 'eyes' of their armies. They flew high above the enemy lines and reported back on such things as troop movements, trench systems and ammunition dumps. Planes were particularly useful during a battle, when they could advise as to whether the enemy was attacking, regrouping and preparing for another attack, or retreating altogether.

DOG FIGHTS

Most of the first airmen were armed with revolvers or machine guns and sometimes they had bombs, which they dropped over the sides of their cockpits. Gradually planes developed into fighting machines. For example, Antony Fokker, a Dutch engineer working for the Germans, invented a mechanism that meant airmen could fire through the blades as the propellers went round. Planes on both sides fired on men in the trenches. Dog fights between fighter planes over the Western Front were common, and some pilots became heroes because of their skill. By the end of the war the 'score' (number of enemy aircraft shot down) for the top pilots was Baron von Richthofen (80), Rene Fonk (75) and Mick Mannock (73). But the reality for most airmen was very different. By 1916, many were young men aged 18, who were given a brief training and sent to war. They could expect to live for three weeks. By 1918, the Great Powers were, altogether, using over 10,000 planes at the front line, and over 50,000 airmen had been killed.

A German fighter plane. This was one of the best dog-fighters of the war.

MACHINE GUNS

All soldiers were given rifles, bayonets and hand grenades, but these were of little use until they had crossed no-man's-land and could actually use them against the enemy. Crossing no-man's-land was the problem. Soldiers moving slowly across open ground were an easy target for machine gunners. Whole **battalions** were killed in this way, and the machine gun proved to be one of the most effective weapons on the Western Front. The British thought little of them at the start of the war. They were heavy, difficult to transport, became too hot inside and often broke down. Soon, however, both sides developed lighter, more reliable machine guns. The British Vickers machine gun, for example, could fire 450–500 bullets a minute over a distance of 2000 m. However, with both sides using similar machine guns, this only added to the stalemate on the Western Front. A breakthrough was urgently needed.

KEY TERM

battalion a large group of soldiers consisting of several companies

ARTILLERY

At the start of the war, all the Great Powers used artillery (mobile field guns). These fired about six shells a minute and were fairly accurate. They were not, however, a lot of use once both sides were dug into trenches along the Western Front. Larger and more powerful guns were developed to bombard enemy lines. The largest gun of all was made by Germany. It was known as 'Big Bertha' and could fire a 108-kilogram shell a distance of 132 km. An artillery attack (called a barrage) on enemy trench systems was not reliable. It was supposed to destroy the barbed wire that protected the trenches, but could go badly wrong. Sometimes, despite hours of artillery fire, the wire was left unbroken, or the ground was turned into mud that could not be crossed. In 1916, the British developed fuse 106 that caused shells to explode parallel to the ground and these proved very effective in cutting barbed wire. By 1917, these fuses were widely used on the Western Front.

GAS

Poison gas was useful as a weapon of war more for the fear it created than the casualties that resulted from its use. The commander of the BEF, Sir John French, said that the use of gas was 'a cynical and barbarous disregard of the well-known usages of civilised war'. But soon both sides were using it. Gas was first used on the Western Front by the Germans at the second battle of Ypres in April 1915. Hundreds of French and Algerian soldiers **suffocated** in thick chlorine gas. Canadians were gassed later that month, and British troops for the first time in May. Soon both sides were using **chlorine**, **phosgene** and **mustard gas**. Gas suffocated and blinded soldiers.

Gas was a terrifying but unreliable weapon. In damp weather, the gas would move slowly around at knee height. If the wind changed direction, troops could end up gassing their own side. A gas alarm system was developed, and troops were supplied with gas masks that they had to put on as soon as the alarm sounded. Sometimes, however, they were not able to put on the gas masks in time. (See Source G.)

SOURCE F

British soldiers, wearing gas masks and firing a Vickers machine gun, at the battle of the Somme in 1916.

EXTEND YOUR KNOWLEDGE

CLARA HABER (1870–1915)

In 1914, a German scientist, Fritz Haber, began experimenting with the ways in which chlorine gas could be used in warfare. His wife Clara, also a scientist, was a **pacifist**. She hated what her husband was doing so much that she committed suicide in protest.

SOURCE G

From a poem by Wilfred Owen. He fought in the trenches and was killed just before the end of the war.

Gas! Gas! Quick, boys! – An ecstasy of fumbling,
Fitting the clumsy helmets just in time;
But someone still was yelling out and stumbling
And flound'ring like a man in fire or lime…
Dim, through misty panes and thick green light,
As under a green sea, I saw him drowning.

SOURCE H

A painting called 'Gassed' by John Singer Sargent. He was sent to France in 1918 by the British government as an official war artist.

EXTEND YOUR KNOWLEDGE

GAS MASKS

The first gas masks were made from cloth soaked in urine (yellow liquid waste that comes out of the body from the bladder). The soldiers hated the smell. Some soldiers found the smell so disgusting that, after a few minutes, they ripped the gas masks off to get some fresh air – and were gassed.

TANKS

The most significant attempt to break the stalemate of trench warfare was the tank. A British army journalist, Lt-Colonel Ernest Swinton, designed an armed vehicle that could cross difficult ground. Fifty tanks made their appearance at the battle of the Somme, but they were not a success. It was a different story in November 1917. At the battle of Cambrai, more than 400 Mark IV tanks smashed their way through the German trenches. In 3 days they had driven 8 km behind the German lines. The German High Command believed that to use tanks was to admit that all proper military tactics had failed. German field commanders, however, were happy to use captured British tanks. German development work was slow, and German tanks did not come into service until March 1918, when it was almost too late.

A British Mark IV tank.

▼ **Figure 3.4** Inside a Mark IV tank

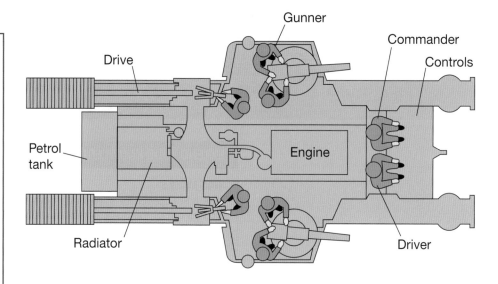

ACTIVITY

1 Explain how artillery firing a barrage could accidentally shell their own side. How was this best avoided?

2 Gas was an unreliable weapon. Why did both sides use it? What do Sources G and H tell you about the effects of gas attacks?

3 Draw three columns. Head the first column 'New weapon', the second column 'Advantages' and the third column 'Disadvantages'. Now fill in the columns. List the new weapons in the first column, their advantages in the second and their disadvantages in the third.

4 Imagine you are a field commander. It is 1916, and you are about to go into battle. Which new technology are you going to depend on most? Write a paragraph to say which it is and explain why.

▼ **Figure 3.5** How a barrage worked

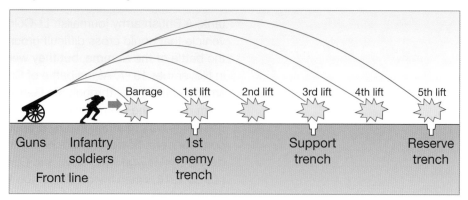

3.4 SUCCESSES AND FAILURES: THE SOMME AND PASSCHENDAELE

LEARNING OBJECTIVES

☐ Understand the significance of the battles of the Somme and Passchendaele

☐ Understand the reasons why neither side was able to claim victory by 1917

☐ Understand the impact of the role of General Haig on strategy and tactics on the Western Front.

THE BATTLE OF THE SOMME, JULY–NOVEMBER 1916

By the end of 1915, the French commander General Joffre, and the British commander General Haig, had agreed on a full-scale attack along the River Somme in the summer of 1916. The first half of the year would be spent developing supplies of men and weapons. However, what they did not realise was that the German Chief of the General Staff, General Falkenhayn, also planned a major attack in 1916. That attack came at Verdun in February 1916.

By July, the Germans had not succeeded in capturing Verdun but they had caused terrible casualties among the French. French soldiers numbering 542,000 were reported killed, wounded or missing; the German casualties were 434,000.

The French were no longer in to position to play a major part in the Somme Offensive that had been planned with Britain for later in 1916 as their forces were still defending Verdun. Indeed, the Somme Offensive was now important not just to try to push through the German lines but also to draw German troops away from Verdun.

SOURCE J

British troops advancing over no-man's-land, 1 July 1916.

General Haig began the Somme Offensive in June 1916, but the Germans were well aware that an attack along the Somme had been planned by Britain and France. German observers in planes and balloons had noted newly constructed roads and railway lines, and they had watched thousands of soldiers arriving with guns, ammunition and supplies. They were not taken by surprise when a massive artillery attack began on 24 June 1916; they were prepared. German troops quickly moved back from the front-line trenches to specially built, strengthened trenches that were more than 12 m deep.

During the Allied bombardment, 1.73 million shells were fired at the German trenches. General Haig believed it had knocked out most of the German front line. He did not know that the bombardment had been shelling empty trenches. The bombardment ended on 1 July and the British troops began crossing no-man's-land. But when the shelling stopped, the Germans raced to their front-line trenches and their machine guns. Haig had ordered 200,000 men to advance toward the German lines that he confidently believed were undefended. Each man was carrying around 30 kg of equipment and they were all ordered to advance slowly towards the enemy.

The first day of the Somme battle was a disaster for the British troops. They were killed in their thousands by German machine guns as they walked across no-man's-land. By nightfall on 1 July, 57,470 Allied and 8000 German soldiers were dead or wounded. General Haig continued. He saw no reason to change his tactics. Between July and November 1916 he ordered attack after attack, always with the same dreadful results. In September, against advice from military experts, he used a new weapon – the tank. Only 50 were ready for war and 29 of these broke down before reaching the battlefield. The rest soon got stuck in the mud. By November, both sides were exhausted. A total of 620,000 Allied and 450,000 German soldiers had been killed or wounded. At most, the Allies had advanced by 15 km along just part of the Western Front.

SOURCE K

A German soldier's eyewitness account of 1 July 1916 on the Somme.

At 7.30 a.m. the hurricane of shells ceased as suddenly as it had begun. Our men at once clambered up the steep shafts leading from the dug-outs. The machine guns were hurriedly put in position. A series of long lines of infantry were seen moving forward from the British trenches. They came on at a steady pace as if expecting to find nothing alive in our front trenches. A few moments later, when the leading British line was within a hundred yards, the rattle of machine-gun fire broke out. Whole sections of the line seemed to fall. All along the line, men could be seen throwing up their arms and collapsing, never to move again.

SOURCE L

Prime Minister David Lloyd George commenting on General Haig.

He had courage and stubbornness. But he did not possess the necessary breadth of vision or imagination to plan a campaign against some of the ablest generals of the war. I never met a man in high position who seemed to me so utterly devoid of imagination.

THE BATTLE OF PASSCHENDAELE, JULY–NOVEMBER 1917

KEY TERM

offensive a planned military attack involving large forces over a long period

General Haig believed that he could break through the German lines in Flanders and aim for the coast. He wanted to capture the naval bases at Blankenberge and Ostend, and make it harder for the Germans to carry out **submarine** attacks on British shipping. (See page 65.) British politicians were doubtful about another major **offensive**. They were anxious not to repeat the terrible casualties of the Somme and they knew that the land over which Haig was proposing to fight was likely to flood. Additionally, German troops were in well-constructed trenches. Nevertheless, Haig won the argument.

The battle of Passchendaele, sometimes called the third battle of Ypres, was a joint British and Canadian offensive, led by General Haig. The battle started on 22 July 1917 with a bombardment of over 4 million shells, which lasted for 10 days and which turned the already wet land into a sea of mud. Haig then ordered the troops to advance. Many found themselves struggling in the mud and filth, some up to their waists in it. Fighting in such conditions was very difficult, if not impossible, and the Allies made slow progress that led to huge casualties.

The bodies of dead men and horses sank in the mud. The battlefield began to smell very bad. The generals in their headquarters 8 km away could smell the rotting men and horses.

The fighting continued for 3 months and battlefield conditions worsened as men, guns and horses sank into the mud before they could be rescued. Finally in November 1917 the Allies were able to capture the village of Passchendaele that had once been behind the German lines. Haig was able to claim victory. Around 240,000 British and 220,000 German soldiers were killed or wounded, and all the Allies had gained was about 800 m of mud. When General Haig sent one of his staff officers to visit the battlefield, the man cried and said, 'My God, did we send men to fight in that?'

SOURCE M

Men carrying a stretcher through the mud of Passchendaele.

GENERAL DOUGLAS HAIG

Haig was the British commander on the Western Front for most of the First World War. He strongly believed that the war would be lost or won there, and this dominated all his thinking. The huge casualties that his military strategy produced have made him a controversial figure. Some regard him as the 'butcher of the Somme', others as 'the man who won the war'.

▶ **Figure 3.6** General Haig

Relieved the pressure on the French at Verdun by starting the Somme Offensive (July 1916)

The battle of Passchendaele (July–November 1917) resulted in heavy casualties but succeeded in weakening the German army

Drew German forces away from the Nivelle offensive by mounting a successful attack on German lines near the town of Arras (April–May 1917)

His strategy resulted in the British army suffering 60,000 casualties on the first day of the battle of the Somme – the most in British history (1 July 1916)

Willing to experiment with the use of tanks to break the stalemate on the Western Front. (Somme 1916 and Cambrai 1917)

Masterminded the British victory at Messines (June 1917)

Haig has been heavily criticised for his role in the war, particularly for the offensives at the Somme and Passchendaele, where the British army suffered such heavy losses. His policy of 'attrition' to wear down the enemy's resources was successful, but at an enormous cost in British lives.

However, it would be wrong to condemn Haig simply because of the high numbers of soldiers lost. The nature of warfare in 1914–18 was always going to result in heavy casualties and Haig's tactics did have some success. The Somme may have been a disaster for the British, but it saved Verdun for the French (which was one of its aims). Haig's calm response to Ludendorff's Offensive resulted in British victories in 1918 which also helped to end the war, when many had expected it to continue into 1919.

Haig was trained as a cavalry man and had a traditional approach to war. At first, he considered the machine gun to be an ineffective weapon, but he was prepared to adopt new methods.

As 1917 ended, there was still stalemate on the Western Front. Little had been gained by either side, and the loss of life had been horrific. In March, revolution had exploded in Russia and the months of trouble that followed led to further revolution in October. In December, Russia signed an armistice with Germany and its allies that took Russia out of the war. Germany could now throw its armies at the Western Front. However, in April, over on the other side of the

Atlantic the USA had declared war on Germany. Men and machines had been arriving on the Western Front within weeks of the American declaration of war. But would enough arrive in time to ensure Allied victory, or would Germany and its allies win? The year 1918 was to be a critical one.

ACTIVITY

1 List the reasons why the battle of the Somme resulted in such a huge loss of life. Is any one reason more important than the others? Explain your answer.
2 It is November 1917. General Haig is planning to attack the Germans at Passchendaele. What advice do you give him?
3 Which side won the battle of the Somme and which side the battle of Passchendaele?

EXTRACT A

From a book by a modern historian, writing about General Haig.

Haig was not deflected from his purpose. Only a man of outstanding honesty and great strength of character would have remained and done what he did. He continued to follow the strategy he believed to be right. The events of 1918 proved it was right. It is doubtful whether anyone else could have done it so well.

EXAM-STYLE QUESTIONS

A03

SKILLS ANALYSIS, ADAPTIVE LEARNING, CREATIVITY

A03 **A04**

SKILLS CRITICAL THINKING, REASONING, DECISION MAKING, ADAPTIVE LEARNING, CREATIVITY, INNOVATION

(a) Study Sources K and L.
How far does Source K support the evidence of Source L about Haig's lack of ability to plan a campaign?
Explain your answer. **(8 marks)**
(b) Study Extract A.
Extract A suggests that Haig was a good general.
How far do you agree with this interpretation?
Use Sources K and L, Extract A and your own knowledge to explain your answer.
(16 marks)

HINT

Don't forget that in question (b) you are being asked whether you agree with the interpretation, not just whether the sources and interpretation do. So you must bring your own knowledge into the answer.

ACTIVITY

1 Draw up a timeline of battles on the Western Front. Use the timeline to write a paragraph explaining why, after three years of fighting, neither side had won.
2 Look at Figure 3.6. Is there anything you think should be added to the information that surrounds the photograph of General Haig? Or is there anything you think should be written differently? For example, you might want to focus more on the numbers of dead and wounded. Sketch out a picture of Haig and add the information around it that you think should be there. Don't just copy out the information provided in Figure 3.6.
3 Draw up two columns. Head one 'Haig the good general' and the other 'Haig the butcher of men'. Find evidence from this section that will help you fill each column. Now use the evidence you have collected to write an answer to the question 'Was Haig a good general?'.

RECAP

RECALL QUIZ

1   What does BEF stand for?
2   Which battle was fought close to Paris, and when?
3   What was a British field postcard?
4   What is the name of the psychological condition that made soldiers shake and moan in fear?
5   Name one type of gas used on the Western Front.
6   What was a barrage?
7   Name the town the French armies were determined to defend at all costs.
8   On what date did the battle of the Somme start?
9   Who was David Lloyd George?
10 When did the battle of Passchendaele begin?

CHECKPOINT

STRENGTHEN

S1 Why was there stalemate on the Western Front by December 1914?
S2 Give two examples of problems faced by soldiers living in trenches.
S3 What was the purpose of a bombardment?

CHALLENGE

C1 Explain how disease became a problem in the trenches.
C2 How important were tanks as a weapon of war?
C3 To what extent was Haig's leadership responsible for the huge number of casualties in (a) the battle of the Somme and (b) the battle of Passchendaele?

SUMMARY

- The Schlieffen Plan failed and Germany had to fight France and Russia at the same time.
- Both sides dug trenches along the Western Front to defend themselves and stop the other side advancing.
- The routine of trench life could become boring when neither side was attacking.
- No-man's-land, between enemy trenches, had to be crossed during an attack. It was full of shell holes and rotting bodies.
- Seriously wounded soldiers were sent to Casualty Clearing Stations or back home.
- Many soldiers suffered from shell-shock.
- Mud, dirt and disease were common problems for all soldiers.
- Both sides used artillery barrages to destroy barbed wire barricades and front line trenches.
- Aircraft were used for observation and later for fighting.
- Machine guns were used by both sides and quickly mowed down lines of advancing troops.
- Poison gas was used by both sides and could blind and suffocate.
- Tanks were first used by the British in November 1917 and by the Germans in March 1918.
- The battle of the Somme lasted for four months; nothing was gained and over a million men were killed or wounded.
- The Allies gained 800 m of mud during the battle of Passchendaele (1917) when nearly half a million men were killed and wounded.
- General Haig was blamed by many for failures on the Western Front.

EXAM GUIDANCE: PARTS (B AND C) QUESTIONS

Part (b)
Study Sources A and B.

SOURCE A

A German soldier's eyewitness account of 1 July 1916 on the Somme.

At 7.30 a.m. the hurricane of shells ceased as suddenly as it had begun. Our men at once clambered up the steep shafts leading from the dug-outs. The German machine guns were hurriedly put in position. A series of long lines of infantry were seen moving forward from the British trenches. They came on at a steady pace as if expecting to find nothing alive in our front trenches. A few moments later, when the leading British line was within a hundred yards, the rattle of machine gun fire broke out. Whole sections of the line seemed to fall. All along the line, men could be seen throwing up their arms and collapsing, never to move again.

SOURCE B

Written by a British soldier who fought on the Somme in July 1916.

We lost as many men on the barbed wire as we did crossing No Man's Land. I think the Germans had been reinforcing their barbed wire before the battle, as it was really difficult to get through. Our generals thought that the artillery bombardment had destroyed the German barbed wire. I can't understand why they thought that. All artillery does to barbed wire is make it even more tangled up. The soldiers all knew that, so why didn't the generals?

A03

SKILLS ANALYSIS, ADAPTIVE LEARNING, CREATIVITY

Question to be answered: How far does Source A support the evidence of Source B about the battle of the Somme in 1916?

Explain your answer.   (8 marks)

Answer

The main area of agreement between the two sources is in the way the Allied forces attacked the German lines (and, therefore why the attacks were unsuccessful). Source A talks about 'the hurricane of shells' ending and after the British advanced 'whole sections of the line seemed to fall'. This is supported in Source B when it says that the British were using artillery fire to smash the German defensive barbed wire, but when they got to German trenches 'we lost as many men on the barbed wire as we did crossing No Man's Land'.

Another area of agreement comes over the defences the Germans had been building. The German soldier (Source A) refers to clambering out of 'steep shafts leading from the dug-outs' and of hurriedly putting machine guns 'in position'. This agrees with Source B where the British soldier says that he thinks the Germans 'had been reinforcing their barbed wire before the battle' and that it was 'really difficult to get through'.

So the sources agree about the tactics, the failure and the preparation.

What are the strengths of this answer?
- *The areas of agreement are clearly identified.*
- *The points made in each paragraph are supported by relevant quotations from both the sources.*

What are the weaknesses?
- *It only does the agreement! That means that, no matter how good the answer is, it cannot score more than 4 marks.*

How do we improve this answer to be one which would get very high marks?
Look at the change to paragraph 3 below.

So the sources agree about the tactics, the failure and the preparation. But they also disagree. Source A gives the impression that the battle was well-planned and was based on a belief in the efficiency of the artillery. It says the barrage stopped and the soldiers 'came on at a steady pace as if expecting to find nothing alive' in the German trenches. So the generals obviously thought artillery was an effective weapon. But the British soldier thinks completely differently. He says that any British soldier could tell them it wouldn't work.

Work with a friend
Discuss whether this answer is likely to get full marks. Use the checklist below. Does the answer now do all four of the things on the list?

☐ Identify similarities
☐ Identify differences
☐ Provide information from the sources to support the statements
☐ Consider the extent of the support/disagreement? Which is stronger?

Part (c)
Study Extract C.

EXTRACT C

From a history of the modern world, published in 2000.

Haig has been heavily criticised for the Somme campaign, which cost so many lives and saw so few gains. However, many historians feel that this is unfair. German accounts from the time show how the German army was seriously weakened by the Allied attack. The Germans called off their Verdun offensive in September 1916 and remained on the defensive throughout 1917. The Somme also saw the introduction of new tactics that were to prove decisive in 1918. The creeping barrage was used for the first time and tanks were also introduced during the Somme.

Question to be answered: Extract C suggests that the criticisms of Haig for the Somme campaign were unfair.

How far do you agree with this interpretation?

Use Extract C, Sources A and B and your own knowledge to explain your answer.   **(16 marks)**

A03   **A04**

SKILLS ▷ CRITICAL THINKING, REASONING, DECISION MAKING, ADAPTIVE LEARNING, CREATIVITY, INNOVATION

Analysis Question 1: What is the question type testing?
In this question, you have to demonstrate that you can use two sources and your own knowledge in order to show how far you agree with a historian's interpretation of an event.

The question will be based on the two contemporary sources you used to answer the (b) question and an additional secondary extract containing a historian's interpretation. They will all be on the same topic.

Analysis Question 2: What do I have to do to answer the question well?
You have to show that you understand the ways in which the two contemporary sources support, or differ from the view given in the extract, and you must use your own knowledge to reach a conclusion about how far you agree with the interpretation.

Analysis Question 3: Are there any techniques I can use to make it very clear that I am doing what is needed to be successful?
■ This is a 16-mark question and you must make sure you write a quick plan before you start. This is because it is important to organise your ideas and your own knowledge.
■ Don't be tempted to write all you know about the topic, but select those parts of your own knowledge that are directly relevant to the interpretation given in the question.

Your answer could look like this.

Paragraph 1: show how the first source supports and disagrees with the interpretation, and use your own knowledge to support this evaluation.

Paragraph 2: show how the second source supports and disagrees with the interpretation and use your own knowledge to support this evaluation.

Paragraph 3: reach an overall judgement that is supported by brief references to the most important points you have made in paragraphs 1 and 2.

Answer

Source A provides evidence to support both sides of the argument. Looking back it seems stupid that the soldiers were advancing at a steady pace instead of running. We know that the Germans were coming out of their deep defences and there was a 'race to parapet' as they hurried to get to their machine guns before the British troops reached the German trenches. So that sounds like something we can criticise Haig for. However, the bombardment had gone on for nearly a week and Haig rightly thought the German trenches would be destroyed. Also, the men were carrying heavy equipment and so running would not have been easy.

Source B says that the German barbed wire was churned up but was just as effective. I think we can blame Haig for that, because if the soldiers knew that artillery didn't destroy wire, then why didn't the Commander-in-Chief? So I don't think the criticism is unfair when it comes to talking about the barbed wire.

However Extract C also provides some extra information which the other sources don't mention. We know that part of the idea of the Somme offensive was to try to stop the Germans attack Verdun. We also know that Haig was using a strategy of attrition on the Somme and the historian seems to be saying that it worked. Britain had just over 400,000 casualties in the Somme campaign, but Germany had 650,000. So that makes it seem like the criticism is unfair.

What are the strengths of this answer?

- *A sound understanding is shown of the two sources*
- *The two sources are clearly linked to different areas of the interpretation, and agreements and disagreements are identified.*
- *Relevant contextual knowledge is used in support of the points made.*
- *The interpretation is challenged by the use of contextual knowledge where it goes beyond the information contained in the sources.*

What are the weaknesses of this answer?

- *The answer looks at the arguments for and against the interpretation using the two sources, own knowledge and the extract itself, but it does not answer the question 'how far?'*
- *To get the very highest marks, the answer has to do more than say 'yes and no'. It has to consider the strength of the argument on each side. For example, it would be impressive to say that Sources A and B show that Haig deserved criticism for the failures on the first day of the Somme, but the Extract is giving a more general picture about the campaign as a whole. So perhaps the criticism of Haig for the campaign itself is unfair.*

Answer checklist

- ☐ Identifies agreement and disagreement with the hypothesis
- ☐ Uses information from the two sources, the extract and own contextual knowledge
- ☐ Addresses 'how far' by 'weighing' the evidence to see which side is most strongly supported.

4. THE WAR AT SEA AND GALLIPOLI

LEARNING OBJECTIVES

- [ ] Understand the impact of the German threat to Britain from the North Sea
- [ ] Understand the significance of the U-boat threat for the conduct of the war
- [ ] Understand the reasons why the Gallipoli campaign was a failure.

The control of the sea was essential to both Britain and Germany if one of them was to win the war. Britain, an island, needed to control the seas so that supplies of food and raw materials could be brought into the country. Britain also needed to control the seas in order to blockade German ports so that supplies could not enter Germany by ship. Germany needed to control the seas so that the German navy could stop supplies of food and raw materials arriving in British ports, and could keep German ports open.

Germany threatened Britain from the North Sea by the use of surface ships, and in the Atlantic by the use of submarines called U-boats. The U-boat threat reduced supplies coming into Britain from the USA, although the U-boat sinking of the liner *Lusitania*, drowning over 100 Americans, nearly brought the USA into the war.

In 1915, the Allies launched an attack on Germany's ally Turkey at Gallipoli. The plan was to clear a route to help provide supplies for Russia. But the Gallipoli campaign was a miserable disaster, mirroring the stalemate on the Western Front.

4.1 THE GERMAN THREAT TO BRITAIN FROM THE NORTH SEA

LEARNING OBJECTIVES

▪ Understand the importance of the battles of Heligoland Bight and Dogger Bank

▪ Understand the impact of the German shelling from the North Sea of mainland Britain

▪ Understand the significance of the battle of Jutland.

KEY TERM

deterrent something that discourages or is intended to discourage an action

▶ **Figure 4.1** The war at sea 1914–18

In 1914, the British navy was the largest in the world; however, during the arms race (see page 12) Germany had built its navy to the point where it was a serious challenge to Britain. Both fleets were strong enough for one to act as a **deterrent** to the other. So Admiral Tirpitz, in command of the German High Seas Fleet, and Admiral Jellicoe, in command of the British Grand Fleet, decided to keep their fleets in port for as long as possible. To lose a major sea battle could have resulted in losing the war. The German High Seas Fleet was anchored in Wilhelmshaven, and the British one in Scapa Flow in the Orkney Islands.

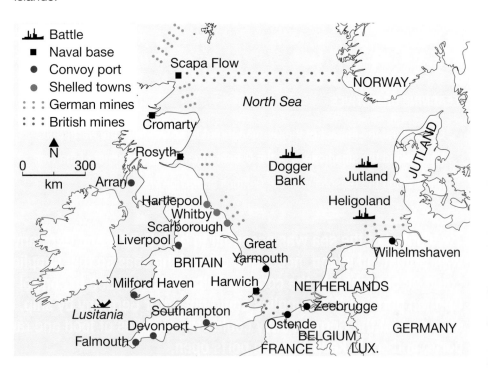

THE BATTLE OF HELIGOLAND BIGHT, 28 AUGUST 1914

Although the large battleships on both sides were kept in port to avoid a major sea battle, smaller warships patrolled the North Sea and there were clashes. One of these clashes was the battle of Heligoland Bight. Two British officers had noticed that German **destroyers** and cruisers had a regular pattern of patrols. The cruisers would go with the destroyers into the North Sea every evening. The destroyers would then patrol the North Sea looking for British shipping, until the morning. The cruisers would meet them and escort them back to port. The British plan was to catch the German destroyers as they returned to port.

A British **squadron** of 31 destroyers, two light cruisers and eight submarines was used to make the attack. The plan was successful. Three German light cruisers and one destroyer were sunk and three more light cruisers were badly damaged. This resulted in the deaths of 712 German sailors, with 530 injured and 336 taken prisoner. On the British side, one light cruiser and three destroyers were damaged, 35 sailors were killed and 40 wounded.

In Britain, cheering crowds regarded the result of the battle as a great victory; in Germany, the reaction was very different. The German Kaiser was horrified at the loss of ships, and issued an order that any future 'decisive action' had to be approved by him in advance. Admiral Tirpitz was very angry. As Admiral of the German High Seas Fleet, he should have the final decision as to whether or not to engage with the enemy. As a result, there was no major fleet action for several months, although small groups of ships were allowed to take part in raids.

EXTEND YOUR KNOWLEDGE

MISSING THE BATTLE
A British submarine, *E4*, fired a torpedo at a German light cruiser, *Stettin*, and missed. The *Stettin* then tried to ram the *E4*. In order to escape, the *E4* dived. When the submarine re-surfaced, all the ships had gone. The battle was over. But the *E4* was able to rescue British and German sailors who were in the sea in lifeboats.

GERMAN RAIDS

German raids on the North Sea coast of Britain had three main objectives:
- to lay down **mines** that would sink passing British ships
- to force British ships to chase the German raiders into waters close to the German coast where German ships would be waiting to ambush them
- to force the British Grand Fleet to split up by sending some of its ships to defend the coastal towns, giving Germany a better chance to catch **isolated** ships and so reduce the strength of the British Grand Feet.

RAID ON GREAT YARMOUTH, 3 NOVEMBER 1914
A squadron of eight German battle cruisers set off across the North Sea, aiming to lay mines in the sea outside Great Yarmouth and shell the town. The gunners' aim was poor and the shells landed on the beach. A fragment from a shell killed one British man. Once the mines were laid, the German ships headed back across the North Sea. British ships that had been patrolling the coast followed them. Despite the fact that one of the German battle cruisers hit two mines and sank with the loss of 235 lives, German commanders saw how easy it was to reach the British coast and were encouraged to try again. British commanders, realising that nothing more serious had happened than a brief and inefficient shelling of a beach, were not alarmed.

RAID ON SCARBOROUGH, WHITBY AND HARTLEPOOL, 16 DECEMBER 1914
The raid on Great Yarmouth had shown the German commanders that fast raids in British waters were possible. They still hoped that raids like that would draw out small sections of the British Grand Fleet, which they could trap and destroy.

British code-breakers were able to read German messages sent between the ships. The British therefore knew that on 15 December a German squadron was heading across the North Sea. The following day, German cruisers began shelling Scarborough. After laying mines, the German ships moved along the coast to Whitby, where the shelling began again. Next came Hartlepool. The whole raid on the three towns lasted little more than 50 minutes before the German ships turned and headed for home. More than a thousand shells were fired, destroying property and killing over a hundred people.

Part of the British Grand Fleet left Scapa Flow in an attempt to stop the German ships. However, the weather was bad and communication between the British ships was confused. There was no decisive, or even significant, battle.

The raids had an enormous impact on British public opinion. The British people were very angry that **civilians** could be attacked in this way, and angered that the British Grand Fleet had seemed to do nothing to prevent the raids. Admiral Jellicoe decided that, in future, the whole British Grand Fleet should be involved in defending Britain's North Sea coast. The British government used the raids as part of their propaganda campaign to encourage men to enlist.

SOURCE A

A British recruitment poster. It is using the horror of Germany bringing the war to mainland Britain to encourage men to join up to defend their country.

MEN OF BRITAIN !
WILL YOU STAND THIS ?

PHOTO. BY F. FOXTON, SCARBOROUGH

Nº 2 Wykeham Street, SCARBOROUGH, after the German bombardment on Decʳ 16ᵗʰ. It was the Home of a Working Man. Four People were killed in this House including the Wife, aged 58, and Two Children, the youngest aged 5.

78 Women & Children were killed and 228 Women & Children were wounded by the German Raiders

ENLIST NOW

THE BATTLE OF DOGGER BANK, 24 JANUARY 1915

The British learned, because they had decoded the signals, that a German raiding squadron was heading for the North Sea coast of Britain. This time they were well prepared. Ships of the British Grand Fleet sailed to meet the German ships close to the **Dogger Bank**.

The German squadron was taken by surprise and turned back to Germany. The British Grand Fleet chased them and started firing, hitting the cruiser *Blücher*. Instead of focusing on the rest of the German squadron, confused signals resulted in the British Grand Fleet concentrating on sinking the *Blücher*. By the time the ship was sunk the rest of the German squadron had escaped. The British did not lose any ships, although 15 men were killed. Germany lost a battle cruiser and 954 men, and so the battle was considered to be a British victory.

SOURCE B

A painting of the battle of Dogger Bank.

THE BATTLE OF JUTLAND, 31 MAY–1 JUNE 1916

On 13 May 1916 came the clash that both sides had feared. The new German admiral, von Scheer, was keen for a **confrontation** and so sent a squadron of ships into the North Sea to draw out the British Grand Fleet. He intended to follow close behind, and make a surprise attack. The British, because they had broken the German codes, knew his ships were coming. They were waiting and ready for an attack. The two great Dreadnought fleets – in total 259 warships carrying over 100,000 men – met off the coast of Denmark at the battle of Jutland.

The fighting was fierce. Most worrying for the British was that the German ships operated better and were less easily damaged than the British ships. When night fell, the Germans suddenly stopped fighting and sailed back to port. It was, however, the British Grand Fleet that had suffered the most damage. The British lost 14 ships and over 6,000 lives, whereas the Germans lost nine ships and over 2,500 men. Both sides claimed victory; Germany because they had sunk more ships, and the British because the German High Seas Fleet was so concerned about its ships being damaged that it never again left port. For Britain, the crucial point was that it remained in control of the North Sea.

SOURCE C

The British Vice-Admiral Beatty, speaking to one of his captains during the battle of Jutland.

Chatfield, there seems to be something wrong with our bloody ships today.

EXTEND YOUR KNOWLEDGE

JACK CORNWELL, 1900–16

Jack Cornwell joined the Royal Navy when he was 15 years old. At the battle of Jutland on 31 May 1916 he was working with one of the guns on *HMS Chester*. All the gun's crew were killed except Jack. When the battle was over, medical officers found him still bravely standing at his post, waiting for orders, although bits of steel were lodged in his chest. He was transferred to hospital on shore and died from his wounds on 2 June 1916, before his mother could arrive at the hospital. He was awarded the Victoria Cross, the highest British award for bravery in battle.

ACTIVITY

1 How would (a) Admiral Tirpitz and (b) Admiral Jellicoe have explained, in 1914, why it was important that their country controlled the North Sea?

2 Draw a chart with three columns.

a Head the columns 'Naval engagement', 'Germany' and 'Britain'. In the first column list the naval battles, including the raids that took place in the North Sea up to the end of 1916. For each one, give a score for Germany and for Britain on a scale of 0 to 10.

b Use the chart to explain why neither navy was able to deliver a knock-out blow.

3 The British government used the German raid on Scarborough to create a recruitment poster. (See Source A.) Use another incident to create your own recruitment poster.

4.2 THE GERMAN THREAT TO BRITAIN FROM UNDER THE SEA

LEARNING OBJECTIVES

■ Understand the importance of submarine warfare

■ Understand the impact of the sinking of the *Lusitania*

■ Understand the ways in which the British navy combatted the U-boat menace.

The war at sea did not only take place in the North Sea. German submarines, operating in the Atlantic Ocean, brought Britain close to defeat. As an island nation, Britain relied heavily on its merchant navy to bring in food and goods from abroad. The Germans planned to use their U-boats to stop this. This meant using U-boats to sink ships that were supplying Britain. Britain imposed a naval blockade on Germany, and on 4 February 1915, the German government announced a submarine blockade of Britain.

SUBMARINE WARFARE, 1915–18

At the start of the war, Germany was not keen to challenge the British Grand Fleet directly. Instead, Tirpitz advised the Kaiser that Germany should use unrestricted submarine warfare as a way of weakening the British war effort. On 4 February 1915, the German government announced that all merchant shipping entering or leaving British waters would be destroyed. This was an ambitious plan. In 1915, Germany had only 21 U-boats and there were about 15,000 sailings in and out of British ports every week. Indeed, only 4 per cent of ships supplying Britain were sunk in 1915.

SOURCE D

A German declaration, 4 February 1915.

All the waters surrounding Great Britain and Ireland, including the whole of the English Channel, are hereby declared a war zone. From 18 February onwards, every merchant vessel found within this war zone will be destroyed.

The problem with unrestricted submarine warfare was that the German U-boats might hit a ship from a neutral country and bring that country into the war on the Allies' side. The one thing that Germany was afraid of was bringing the USA into the war on the same side as Britain, France and Russia. This very nearly happened in May 1915, when a German U-boat sank the US passenger ship, the *Lusitania*. (See page 67.) The US government was angered by this attack on a neutral passenger liner, and came close to declaring war on Germany. It issued a strong protest to Germany, and this resulted in Germany temporarily stopping its policy of unrestricted warfare. In September 1915 and again in May 1916, Germany stated that its U-boats would not attack neutral shipping. These promises did not end submarine warfare, but they reduced its effectiveness.

By 1917, however, the German U-boat fleet had increased to almost 200. Germany believed that Britain could be starved into submission, and so restarted its campaign of unrestricted submarine warfare. At first, the U-boats

SOURCE E

A German U-boat.

did well and they sank 841,114 tonnes of Allied shipping. Merchant ships left ports with their captains knowing that one in four ships would not reach their destination. However, an effective rationing system meant that Britain did not starve. It was also true that British measures meant the German U-boat fleet could not continue with its early successes.

ANTI-U-BOAT MEASURES

- Huge minefields were set in the English Channel. An explosion was caused if a U-boat touched one. They were very effective.
- **Depth charges** were developed. They exploded and destroyed submarines if they were dropped from ships close by.
- The British prime minister, David Lloyd George, persuaded the Royal Navy to use a convoy system. Merchant ships carrying supplies across the Atlantic sailed in groups that were protected by the Royal Navy.
- The British introduced Q-ships. These were ships that were armed, but which were disguised by making them look like merchant ships. U-boats got a nasty shock when they attacked.

KEY TERM

depth charge a bomb that explodes at a particular depth under water

LORD HERBERT HORATIO KITCHENER, 1850–1916

Lord Kitchener was British Secretary of State for War and is best known as the face on the 'Your Country Needs You' poster. In May 1916, Tsar Nicholas II invited Kitchener to visit Russia to advise him on military matters. On 5 June, Kitchener set sail from Scapa Flow on the battle cruiser *HMS Hampshire*, bound for the Russian port of Archangel. After a few hours at sea, the ship hit a German mine and sank in 15 minutes. Kitchener was among the 643 men who drowned. His body was never recovered.

The anti-U-boat measures were highly successful.

- Large numbers of U-boats were sunk by mines. For example, 20 out of the 63 U-boats that were sunk in 1917 were destroyed because they had hit a mine.
- Between 1915 and the end of 1917, depth charges destroyed only five submarines. However, an improved design meant that the following year, depth charges destroyed 22 U-boats.
- The first convoy crossed the Atlantic on 10 May 1917. By 1918, only 1 per cent of ships in convoys were sunk by U-boats.
- Q-ships were responsible for about 10 per cent of all U-boats sunk.

By mid-1918, U-boat losses had become so great that they could not operate successfully. By this time, too, the **morale** of U-boat crews was very low. There were plans to combine U-boats into groups so that they could hunt for Allied shipping in packs, but by the middle of 1918 there were not enough U-boats to do this. Plans to build more were prevented by lack of materials, shipbuilders and time. On 24 October 1918, all U-boats returned to their home ports in Germany and never fought again.

THE SINKING OF THE *LUSITANIA*, 7 MAY 1915

On 1 May 1915, the British luxury liner, the *Lusitania*, set sail from New York bound for Liverpool. The German embassy had warned in February that any ship entering the war zone around Britain and Ireland could be sunk, and a special warning was printed in American newspapers beside an advertisement for the trip to Liverpool.

SOURCE F

A warning from the German embassy, printed in US newspapers beside Cunard's advertisement of the voyage of the *Lusitania*.

Travellers intending to embark on the Atlantic voyage are reminded that a state of war exists between Germany and her allies and Great Britain and her allies; that the zone of war includes the waters adjacent to the British Isles; that, in accordance with formal notice given by the Imperial German Government, vessels flying the flag of Great Britain or of any of her allies, are liable to destruction in those waters and that travellers sailing in the war zone on ships of Great Britain or her allies, do so at their own risk.

However, as the fastest ship in the world, many passengers must have believed that the *Lusitania* could sail faster than any submarine. They had not considered a submarine's torpedoes. On 7 May, when the ship was 13 km off the coast of Ireland, the German submarine *U20* torpedoed the *Lusitania*. A second, unexplained internal explosion, together with the torpedo, sank the *Lusitania* in 18 minutes and most passengers did not stand a chance. The ship tilted so much as it went down that many of the lifeboats could not be launched. Some hit passengers crowding the decks and others dropped their passengers into the sea. Of the 1959 passengers on board, 1198 drowned; 128 of them were Americans.

SOURCE G

A painting of the sinking of the *Lusitania* on 7 May 1915.

EXTEND YOUR KNOWLEDGE

TRYING TO SAVE BABIES

Arthur Vanderbilt, who was one of the world's richest men, and Carl Frohman, who wrote successful plays, were on board the ship. They tried to save some babies that were being looked after in the *Lusitania*'s nursery. When the ship began to sink, they rushed to help. Once in the nursery, they tied life jackets to the babies' cots, hoping that this would keep them afloat in the sea. This very nearly worked. The cots, with the babies tucked inside, floated off the ship when the waters rose. But they were all pulled under and drowned when the *Lusitania* sank beneath the surface of the sea. The two men who tried to save them drowned, too.

The sinking led to international anger, especially in Britain and America. A British newspaper, the *Daily Express*, claimed, 'It is simply an act of piracy. Nothing more.' There were calls for the USA to declare war on Germany. Germany responded by publishing a statement saying that because the *Lusitania* carried war materials, Germany had the right to destroy the ship even though there were passengers on board.

SOURCE H

The headline and photograph in a British newspaper, the *Daily Mail*, Monday 10 May 1915.

The British government denied that the ship was carrying war materials, but there were some unusual things about the *Lusitania*.

- On 12 May 1913, in strict secrecy, one of the *Lusitania*'s decks was converted to a gun deck that could take six guns on each side, capable of firing high explosive shells.
- Part of the *Lusitania*'s cargo consisted of:
  - 4,927 boxes of cartridges
  - 1,248 cases of 3-inch filled shrapnel shells
  - 18 cases of fuses for artillery shells
  - a large quantity of gun cotton, an explosive used in the manufacture of shells
  - two consignments, labelled 'butter' and 'cheese', that were unrefrigerated and together weighed 90 tonnes.

SOURCE I

Official note sent to Germany by the US government after the sinking.

Whatever the facts regarding the *Lusitania*, the principal fact is that a great steamer, primarily and chiefly a conveyance for passengers, and carrying a thousand souls who had no part or lot in the conduct of the war, was torpedoed and sunk without so much as a challenge or warning, and that men, women and children were sent to their death in circumstances unparalleled in modern warfare.

EXAM-STYLE QUESTION

A03

SKILLS   ANALYSIS, ADAPTIVE LEARNING, CREATIVITY

Study Sources F and I.

How far does Source F support the evidence of Source I about the sinking of the *Lusitania*?

Explain your answer. **(8 marks)**

HINT

Think about whether or not a warning was given by Germany.

ACTIVITY

1 Give one reason why unrestricted German submarine warfare could damage the British war effort. Give one reason why unrestricted German submarine warfare could be a risky strategy for Germany.
2 Imagine you are a journalist working for the *Daily Mail* in May 1915. Use the information in this section to write the story that could have come under the headline in Source H.
3 Look at Source E.
  a What can you learn about the U-boat menace?
  b Write a paragraph to explain how Britain overcame the U-boat menace.

4.3 THE GALLIPOLI CAMPAIGN

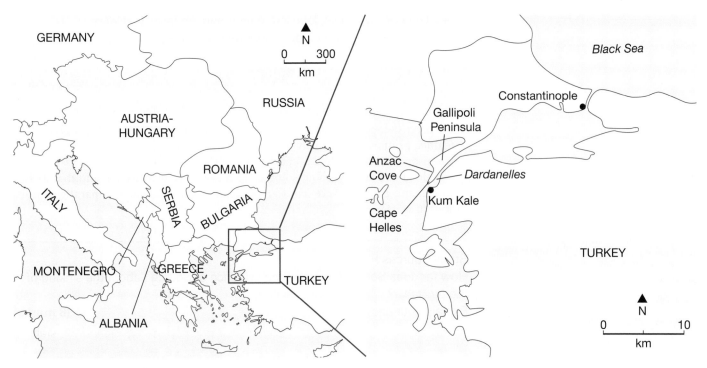

▲ **Figure 4.2** Gallipoli campaign

THE REASONS FOR THE GALLIPOLI CAMPAIGN

In October 1914, Turkey joined the war on the side of Germany and Austria-Hungary. This gave the Allies a serious problem. Turkey (see Figure 4.2) controlled the Dardanelles, a narrow strait of water leading to the Black Sea. This meant that supplies of food and arms could no longer be sent to Russia via the Mediterranean Sea. It also meant that Russian ships, moored in the Black Sea, were trapped. Added to this, there was stalemate on the Western Front (see page 38) and Russia, desperate for help, was being attacked by Germany and Austria-Hungary.

CHURCHILL'S GALLIPOLI PLAN

Winston Churchill, the British First Lord of the Admiralty, made a plan that would move enemy forces away from Russia and open the Dardanelles to British and French shipping. Churchill's plan was straightforward. A naval bombardment would knock out the Turkish forts on the Gallipoli peninsula that were guarding the Dardanelles. This would enable ground troops to move in and clear the way, opening the Dardanelles to Allied shipping and providing food and arms to Russia.

▼ **Figure 4.3** Churchill's Gallipoli plan

Allied troops attack Turkey by invading the Gallipoli peninsula at the entrance to the Dardanelles.

The Allied invasion draws German and Austro-Hungarian troops away from attacking Russia to defending Turkey.

The Allies win control of the Gallipoli peninsula.

Allied troops clear the Dardanelles of mines and open the straits to Allied shipping.

Supplies of food and arms are taken into Russia through the Mediterranean Sea and the Dardanelles.

Allied forces attack the Turkish capital, Constantinople.

Constantinople falls to the Allies and Turkey leaves the war.

Churchill's plan was bold and simple. But would it work? If it did, there was every chance that neighbouring neutral countries, such as Bulgaria and Greece, would join the war on the Allied side. They would see that the Allies were militarily superior and would want to be on the winning side. This would make the Allied forces too strong for Austria-Hungary, and they would be forced out of the war, leaving Germany to fight on alone. In this situation, Germany would lose the war. However, if the plan failed, thousands of lives would be lost with nothing gained.

MAIN FEATURES OF THE GALLIPOLI CAMPAIGN

■ On 19 February 1915, an Anglo-French naval force began bombarding Turkish guns that were placed along the coast. The bombardment destroyed some forts, and on 18 March the main attack was launched. Eighteen battleships, supported by cruisers and destroyers, tried to force their way through the Dardanelles. But three battleships were blown up by mines, 300 sailors drowned and the rest of the fleet rapidly retreated.

■ It was then decided that an Allied army would be landed on the coast of Gallipoli. Their job would be to capture the forts guarding the entrance to the Dardanelles so that the waters of the straits could be cleared of mines.

■ On 25 April 1915, the Allied troops, mainly British and Anzac (Australian and New Zealand Army Corps) soldiers with some French support, commanded by General Ian Hamilton, invaded the Gallipoli peninsula. However:
  – the troops had no experience of landing on enemy beaches
  – most of the Turkish beaches were below cliffs and steeply rising ground
  – Hamilton did not have up-to-date maps of the area.

■ The Turks were prepared for the attack. They had spent the time between February and April strengthening their positions and making sure their guns were ready for action.

■ Anzac troops landed at what was later called Anzac Cove. They were hit by machine-gun fire as they left their landing boats. They managed to establish themselves in Anzac Cove but were never able to move inland. Later, the Anzacs attempted another landing at Sulva Bay. Although their landing was unopposed, after a couple of days they were met with fierce fire from the Turks, and could not advance further.

SOURCE J

Anzac troops landing at Anzac Cove in the summer of 1915. The barrels contain fresh water.

A New Zealand soldier describes the landing at Anzac Cove.

The whole beach went up in flames in front of us. Bullets hit us like a blizzard of lead. The boat next to us was torn apart – bodies, blood, splinters of wood. Bodies jammed in so tight in other small boats they couldn't even fall over.

- The French landed at Kum Kale and were defeated after a day's heavy fighting. The soldiers who remained were taken off by French ships.
- The British landed at Cape Helles. The beaches quickly became bloodbaths. Although they managed to gain a small piece of land on the shore, and despite fighting several battles, the British never captured a single Turkish fort.

An Australian soldier describes what it was like trying to fight his way inland, up the cliffs, after landing at Anzac Cove.

There was an awful tornado of shrapnel from the Turkish fort as they unmercifully shelled the seashore. We dared not fire because of our own men being often in front of us, and the nature of the ground making it impossible to get into a line and charge. When we got half way up, we thought we could have a bit of a rest. So we sat down for a bit and those who were lucky enough to find that their pipe, cigarettes and tobacco were dry, had a good smoke.

The British and Anzac troops were forced to dig trenches in order to protect themselves from Turkish fire. They could not advance and take the Turkish forts that would enable them to clear the Dardanelles straits of enemy mines. The Gallipoli campaign had been planned to end the stalemate on the Western Front. Now it looked very similar to the Western Front, with the same stalemate, the same trenches and the same suffering, casualties and death.

EVACUATION

By the autumn of 1915, it was obvious that the campaign had failed. General Hamilton was told about a government plan to end the campaign and evacuate all the troops. He strongly opposed this, claiming that casualties during an evacuation could be as high as 50 per cent. He was removed as commander-in-chief. His replacement, General Monro, toured the beaches of Gallipoli and quickly realised that the situation was impossible. He ordered an immediate evacuation.

Between 10 December 1915 and 9 January 1916, over 135,000 troops and 300 guns were evacuated from Gallipoli and Hellas. Careful efforts had been taken to make the Turkish troops believe that nothing out of the ordinary was happening. For example, rifles were set up so that they fired at certain times without a soldier being near. This would convince the Turks that there were still troops in position. The evacuation was easily the most successful part of the campaign. The men and weapons were taken away without the Turkish army noticing, and only three casualties were officially recorded.

THE EFFECTS OF THE CAMPAIGN
- Altogether, 480,000 Allied troops took part in the campaign. A total of 204,000 men were wounded and 48,000 killed.
- Many soldiers became sick because of the dirty conditions. Typhoid, dysentery and diarrhoea were common illnesses. It is estimated that around 145,000 British soldiers and 64,000 Turkish soldiers were affected.
- The Dardanelles were still closed to Russian ships and Russia faced the prospect of slow starvation.
- The stalemate on the Western Front was not broken, and troops had been moved away from the Western Front where they were desperately needed.

- Germany was able to strengthen its position on the Western Front
- Turkish morale was high and its troops confident.
- General Hamilton was removed from his command and his career was further damaged by Winston Churchill's comment, 'He came, he saw, he capitulated [surrendered].'
- Winston Churchill's career was also damaged: he was forced to resign as First Lord of the Admiralty.

ACTIVITY

1 Study Churchill's Gallipoli plan (see Figure 4.3). With a partner, work out the weak points in the plan. Compare your findings with others in your class. How would you have advised Churchill to plan differently?
2 Look carefully at Source J. Make a list of the problems the Anzac troops seem to be facing.
3 Write a paragraph explaining why the Gallipoli campaign failed.
4 What, in your view, was the most serious outcome of the failed campaign? Explain your answer.

EXTRACT A

From a modern historian, writing about the Gallipoli campaign.

Away from Europe, the joint landings at Gallipoli were well thought out but poor in operation.

ACTIVITY

1 Explain why control of the seas around Britain was important (a) for Germany and (b) for Britain.
2 Draw a timeline of the activities of the British navy in the North Sea, the Atlantic Ocean and at Gallipoli. Beside each activity, write a sentence to say whether or not the British navy was successful.
3 By the end of 1915, there was stalemate on the Western Front and stalemate on the Gallipoli peninsula. Did these happen for the same reasons? Explain your answer.

EXAM-STYLE QUESTIONS

A01

SKILLS ▶ ANALYSIS, ADAPTIVE LEARNING, CREATIVITY

Study Sources K and L.
How far does Source K support the evidence of Source L about the Anzac invasion of Gallipoli?
Explain your answer.   **(8 marks)**

HINT

Think about whether one source was describing something more dangerous than the other one.

RECAP

RECALL QUIZ

1 Name the admiral leading the British Grand Fleet in 1914.
2 When was the battle of Heligoland Bight?
3 Who was leading the German High Seas Fleet in 1914?
4 Name two British towns that were shelled from the sea by the German navy.
5 Which battle happened between 31 May and 1 June 1916?
6 What was unrestricted submarine warfare?
7 Where and when was the liner *Lusitania* sunk?
8 What does Anzac stand for?
9 When did the invasion of the Gallipoli peninsula start?
10 Who was the British First Lord of the Admiralty during the Gallipoli campaign?

CHECKPOINT

STRENGTHEN

S1 Give two examples of British naval successes in the First World War.
S2 Why did a German U-boat sink the *Lusitania*?
S3 Re-read the information about the Gallipoli campaign. Identify one reason for the campaign, one event of the campaign and one consequence.

CHALLENGE

C1 If both the Germans and the British thought they had such wonderful navies, why was there only one major sea battle in the war?
C2 Why were the U-boats, in the end, unsuccessful in the battle of the Atlantic?
C3 To what extent was the failure of the Gallipoli campaign due to poor planning, or to problems in carrying out the plans?

SUMMARY

- Britain needed to control the seas so that supplies could be brought in.
- Germany needed to control the seas in order to defeat Britain.
- The battles of Heligoland Bight (August 1914) and Dogger Bank (January 1915) were British victories.
- German ships shelled towns on the east coast of Britain.
- During the battle of Jutland (May–June 1916), British ships were more damaged than German ones.
- After the battle of Jutland, the German High Seas Fleet sailed back to port and stayed there for the rest of the war.
- In 1915, Germany began unrestricted submarine warfare.
- A U-boat sank the passenger ship *Lusitania* in May 1915, which nearly brought the USA into the war.
- The British convoy system, mines and Q-boats defeated the U-boat menace.
- A British naval bombardment (February 1915) failed to destroy Turkish forts on the Gallipoli peninsula and open the Dardanelles sea route to Russia.
- British and Anzac troops landed on the Gallipoli peninsula, but failed to destroy the Turkish forts.
- British and Anzac troops were evacuated from Gallipoli.
- Churchill was blamed for the failure of the campaign.

EXAM GUIDANCE: PART (B) QUESTIONS

Study Sources A and B.

SOURCE A

A warning from the German Embassy, printed in April 1915 in US newspapers beside Cunard's advertisement of the voyage of the *Lusitania*.

Travellers intending to embark on the Atlantic voyage are reminded that a state of war exists between Germany and her allies and Great Britain and her allies; that the zone of war includes the waters adjacent to the British Isles; that in accordance with formal notice given by the Imperial German Government, vessels flying the flag of Great Britain or any of her allies, are liable to destruction in those waters and that travellers sailing in the war zone on ships of Great Britain or her allies, do so at their own risk.

SOURCE B

The official note sent to Germany by the US government after the sinking of the *Lusitania* in May 1915.

Whatever the facts regarding the *Lusitania*, the principal fact is that a great steamer, primarily and chiefly a conveyance for passengers, and carrying a thousand souls who had no part or lot in the conduct of the war, was torpedoed and sunk without so much as a challenge or warning, and that men, women and children were sent to their death in circumstances unparalleled in modern warfare.

A03

SKILLS ANALYSIS, ADAPTIVE LEARNING, CREATIVITY

Question to be answered: How far does Source A support the evidence of Source B about the sinking of the *Lusitania* in May 1915?

Explain your answer.   (8 marks)

1 ▶ **Analysis Question 1: What is the question type testing?**
In this question, you have to demonstrate that you can comprehend, interpret and cross-refer sources. In this question, that means you can see similarity and difference between two sources in what they say about the sinking of the *Lusitania*.

2 ▶ **Analysis Question 2: What do I have to do to answer the question well?**
You have to write about points and areas of agreement and difference between the two sources that you are given. Don't be tempted to tell the examiner what each source says. The examiner will already know that! Go straight for the agreements and differences. You might, for example, say 'The main areas of agreement between the two sources are …' or 'The sources both agree that …' or 'The two sources differ about …'.

3 ▶ **Analysis Question 3: Are there any techniques I can use to make it very clear that I am doing what is needed to be successful?**
This is an 8-mark question, and you need to be sure you leave enough time to answer the (c) part, which is worth 16 marks. So you need to get straight in to your answer. Divide it into three parts. In the first paragraph, identify areas and points of agreement; in the second paragraph, do the same but identify differences. Remember to quote from the source material to support what you are saying. Your final paragraph should explain the extent of the support or agreement between the two sources. That means, how strongly they agree or disagree.

You must identify both agreement and difference. You will get up to 5 marks for doing this and for supporting what you have selected with material from the sources (but a maximum of 4 if you do 'just one side'). There are 3 additional marks for explaining the extent to which one source supports the other.

Answer

The sources both agree on their main subject area, which is that there was some danger relating to the passenger liner the Lusitania. Source A was printed beside Cunard's advertisement about the transatlantic voyage of the ship and warns that Allied passenger liners that were sailing in 'the zone of war' which 'includes the waters adjacent to the British Isles' could be sunk. Source B tells us that the Lusitania was a passenger liner and that it was torpedoed.

The two sources differ in one important area. Source B makes it clear that the Lusitania was sunk 'without so much as a challenge or a warning'. But the whole of Source A is the warning when it says 'vessels flying the flag of Great Britain or any of her allies, are liable to destruction'. Source A is saying that any ship carrying the British flag, or one of its allies, and entering the war zone is in danger. So the sinking was legitimate. Source B says the ship and passengers 'had no part or lot in the conduct of the war'. So the sinking was not legitimate.

In conclusion, Source A supports the evidence of Source B only in as far as they are both referring to the sinking of the Lusitania. However, the lack of support is huge. Source A is a warning that allied shipping will risk being sunk, and Source B denies the existence of any such warning and believes the sinking to be unjust. It is interesting, though, that Source B also say 'Whatever the facts regarding the Lusitania'. That might mean the US government knew there was a risk. So the sources might not be disagreeing as strongly as it seems at first.

What are the strengths of this answer?

- *The agreements and differences between the sources are clearly identified in separate paragraphs.*
- *The points made in each paragraph are supported by appropriate quotations from the sources.*
- *The conclusion looks at the extent of support Source A gives to Source B.*
- *The comment about 'Whatever the facts regarding the Lusitania' is very perceptive.*

What are the weaknesses of this answer?

- *There are no real weaknesses here, and this is the way to answer such questions. The student just needs to be sure that the answer can be given in no more than 10–15 minutes.*

Answer checklist

- ☐ Identifies similarities
- ☐ Identifies differences
- ☐ Provides information from the sources to support the statements
- ☐ Considers the extent of the support/disagreement. Which is stronger?

5. THE DEFEAT OF GERMANY

LEARNING OBJECTIVES

- Understand the key factors of the Ludendorff Offensive in the spring of 1918
- Understand the significance of the US entry into the war
- Understand the reasons why Germany lost the First World War.

The year 1918 was a critical one for the conduct of the war. In the spring, German General Ludendorff launched an offensive that was to be Germany's last, desperate attempt to win the war before US troops arrived in Europe to support the Allies. At first, the offensive seemed successful. German troops pushed into France and got within shelling distance of Paris. But they had gone too far, too fast. Supplies could not keep up with the pace of the advance. The Allies retreated and waited. They restructured their armies under the overall control of French General Foch, developed new tactics and learned how to use technology to help make an attack successful. In August the Allies, strengthened by US soldiers, launched their Hundred Days' Offensive. They smashed through the German lines, forcing the German armies to retreat until they were finally back behind the Hindenburg Line and into Germany. An armistice was agreed between Germany and the Allies, and on the 11th hour of the 11th month, 1918, all fighting on the Western Front stopped.

5.1 THE LUDENDORFF OFFENSIVE, SPRING 1918

LEARNING OBJECTIVES

- Understand why Ludendorff launched a German offensive in the spring of 1918
- Understand the early successes of the offensive
- Understand the reasons why the offensive finally failed.

Significant events occurred in both the USA and Russia in 1917 and 1918. The events were not linked, but together they helped to end the war and defeat Germany.

On 6 April 1917, the USA declared war on Germany. This was partly due to Germany restarting its policy of unrestricted submarine warfare (see pages 65–69) and partly because of the Zimmermann telegram that was published in US newspapers. This was a coded telegram sent by the German Foreign Secretary, Arthur Zimmermann, to the German ambassador to Mexico on 11 January 1917. The German government thought the USA was going to join the war. So they wanted to persuade Mexico to invade the USA if that happened. The Germans offered to provide military and financial support and help Mexico take over territory in Texas, New Mexico and Arizona. Such an invasion would delay the sending of US troops to Europe and give Germany a good chance of winning the war. The government of Mexico, however, did not agree.

In February and October 1917 there were two revolutions in Russia. The first revolution removed the tsar, Nicholas II, from power. The provisional government that was created to rule Russia in his place continued the war. A new attack on Germany was at first successful, but then the German **counter-attack** defeated the Russian troops. Thousands of Russian soldiers deserted. In this chaos, there was a second revolution. Lenin set up a **Bolshevik** government that had promised to end the war with Germany. On 3 March 1917, Russia signed a peace treaty with Germany, the Treaty of Brest-Litovsk. Russia was out of the war.

THE NEED FOR GERMAN ACTION

The German Kaiser and the German High Command realised that they needed to take action as soon as possible.
- The USA had declared war on Germany. However, American troops had to be transported across the Atlantic Ocean and they had to be trained in the type of fighting they would experience on the Western Front. This would take time. Germany needed to win the war before the American troops made a real difference to the Allied fighting forces.
- War against the Russians on the Eastern Front had ended, and Germany had transferred 500,000 men to the Western Front. The time had come to use them.
- General Ludendorff chose the day of 21 March 1918 for his offensive.

OPERATION MICHAEL, MARCH–JULY 1918

General Ludendorff launched his great and final offensive – Operation Michael – on 21 March 1918.

GERMAN ACTION

Ludendorff planned to break the stalemate on the Western Front by driving west through the weakest part of the French and British lines of trenches. Before dawn on 21 March, suddenly, 600 German guns began a powerful bombardment of enemy trenches that lasted for 5 hours. This was followed by the releasing of clouds of deadly mustard gas that suffocated the British soldiers in their trenches. Instead of following up the bombardment with waves of infantry, as was usual and which the British would be expecting, Ludendorff used a different strategy. Specially trained and lightly armed small bands of 'storm troopers' advanced quickly along the whole front line. Luckily for them, they were hidden in a thick fog as they focused on breaking through gaps and weak defences. Confused and disoriented, the British climbed out of their trenches, and retreated. Thousands surrendered or were taken prisoner of war.

EXTEND YOUR KNOWLEDGE

PRISONERS OF WAR

During the First World War, around 10 million people were captured. Most were servicemen, but some were civilians. They were sent to detention camps until the war ended. The countries holding prisoners of war sent lists of their prisoners to the International Red Cross. The International Red Cross informed the prisoners' relatives that they were safe.

SOURCE A

A British soldier remembers the German attack in March 1918.

As the fog cleared a little, we saw the Germans for the first time advancing in thousands. The whole area was darkened by their figures, a moving mass of grey. The ground helped their advance; it was a maze of shell holes and they crawled from one to the other. All our guns, damaged by earlier shell-fire, were out of action, and by now German bullets were whistling at us from all directions. It was only then that we realised that we were completely surrounded and hopelessly outnumbered.

SOURCE B

Specially trained German storm troops, wearing gas masks, attack Allied positions through thick woods.

Close to 100,000 German infantrymen followed the storm troopers and took control of the land gained, despite some fierce opposition from Allied forces. At first, this strategy was brilliantly successful. By July, German troops had advanced 65 km into France. They had crossed the River Somme and had reached the banks of the River Marne. Paris was within range of heavy gunfire.

▼ **Figure 5.1** The Ludendorff Offensive

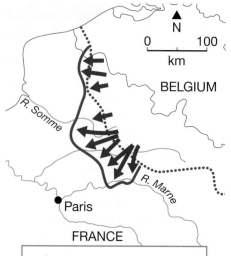

German attacks

The furthest limit of the German advance

The trench lines before the offensive

For the second time in the war, it looked as though Paris would fall to the Germans. However, an important part was played by about 20,000 newly arrived American soldiers. (See page 82.) Fighting with the Allies, they helped to stop the German advance at the second battle of the Marne in July 1918.

ALLIED REACTION

British and French leaders decided to put all the Allied forces under the overall command of General Foch. A French general, his task was to make sure that all the Allied armies acted as a single force and not as separate units. Each national army kept its own commanders-in-chief, although they all worked under General Foch. At first, even though the Germans had been stopped at the Marne, it seemed that the combined Allied forces could do little to stop the German advance.

SOURCE C

A 'Special Order of the Day' issued to British troops on 11 April 1918 by Field Marshal Sir Douglas Haig, the commander-in-chief of the British armies in France.

Three weeks ago today the enemy began his terrific attacks against us on a fifty-mile front. His objects are to separate us from the French, to take the Channel Ports and destroy the British army.

In spite of throwing already 106 Divisions into the battle and enduring the most reckless sacrifices of human life, he has as yet made little progress towards his goals.

We owe this to the determined fighting and self-sacrifice of our troops. Words fail me to express the admiration which I feel for the splendid resistance offered by all ranks of our Army under the most trying circumstances.

Many amongst us are now tired. To those I would say that Victory will belong to the side that holds out the longest. The French army is moving rapidly and in great force to our support.

There is no other course open to us but to fight it out. Every position must be held to the last man: there must be no retirement. With our backs to the wall and believing in the justice of our cause, each one of us must fight on to the end. The safety of our homes and the Freedom of mankind alike depend upon the conduct of each one of us at this critical moment.

THE FAILURE OF THE LUDENDORFF OFFENSIVE

It may have looked as if the Ludendorff Offensive had been a success. Allied forces were in retreat; German troops were 65 km inside France and were now in a position to attack Paris. Perhaps above all, the offensive had broken the stalemate of trench warfare. What could possibly go wrong?

- Ludendorff had sent too many men into French territory, where 400,000 had been killed, and those that remained were exhausted. He did not have enough troops in reserve to back up or replace his forces in France.
- The German troops had gone too far and too fast into French territory. It had not been possible for supplies to keep pace with them. The men were hungry and short of replacement weapons and ammunition. They had to **loot** food and supplies from captured enemy trenches and French villages. The supply lines that did exist were long and could be easily disrupted by the Allies.

■ The German advance into France had created a 'salient', or bulge, that was 130 km long and 65 km wide. (See Figure 5.1.) It could be attacked from three sides and so the German troops were open to attack.

ACTIVITY

1 Imagine you are one of Ludendorff''s advisors. There is a short period between Russia leaving the war and American troops arriving on the Western Front. What do you advise him to do? With a partner, decide not only on the advice, but also on how it should be carried out.

2 Draw a flow chart of the Ludendorff Offensive. Start with the bombardment and end with Paris being within range of German heavy gunfire. Write a short paragraph explaining which point was the most significant in breaking the stalemate on the Western Front.

3 Read Source C.

  a Why did 'the enemy' begin 'terrific attacks' against the Allies three weeks before the order was made?

  b Do you agree with Haig's statement that the enemy 'has as yet made little progress'? Explain your answer.

  c Some British soldiers found the 'Special Order of the Day' inspiring; others found it depressing. Find one sentence that a soldier would find inspiring and one that another soldier would find depressing.

  d Using just the content of Source C, explain whether or not you think Haig expected to lose the war.

4 Read the section headed 'The failure of the Ludendorff Offensive'. Which of the three reasons do you think was the most important in bringing about failure? Explain your answer.

5.2 THE ALLIED DRIVE TO VICTORY, JULY–NOVEMBER 1918

LEARNING OBJECTIVES

■ Understand the impact of US entry into the war

■ Understand the ways in which the Allies changed their strategy to make use of new technology

■ Understand the importance of the Hundred Days' counter-attack by the Allies.

A combination of the arrival of US troops in Europe and the regrouping of Allied armed forces using different tactics following the collapse of the Ludendorff Offensive led to the final defeat of Germany.

THE ENTRY OF THE USA INTO THE WAR

The USA had remained neutral before its official declaration of war in April 1917. Nevertheless, it had supplied Britain and other allies with money, food, raw materials and arms. Once war was declared, these supplies were increased considerably and were no longer secret. After April 1917, the USA sent thousands of armed forces across the Atlantic. By the time of the armistice in November 1918, there were almost 2 million American soldiers in Europe.

SOURCE D

An American song, written in 1917.

Over there, over there
Send the word, send the word, over there.
That the Yanks are coming, the Yanks are coming,
The drums rum-tumming everywhere.
So prepare, say a prayer,
Send the word, send the word to beware.
We'll be over, we're coming over,
And we won't come back till it's over, over there.

EXTEND YOUR KNOWLEDGE

DOUGHBOYS
Doughboy was the nickname given to US soldiers. No one knows exactly where this nickname came from. It might have started during the Mexican war (1846–48), where US troops made long marches across dusty land, which made them look as if they had been covered in flour, or dough. The name could also have referred to the soldiers' white belts that they cleaned with dough, or to the fried dough balls that the soldiers liked to eat.

AMERICAN FORCES ON THE WESTERN FRONT

The US President, Woodrow Wilson, put Major-General John Pershing in command of the American Expeditionary Force (the AEF) sent to Europe. Few American soldiers had fought in any wars, and they were certainly not familiar with the sort of conditions they would find on the Western Front. Pershing therefore insisted that American forces were well trained before going to Europe and, later, many received further training once they arrived in France. The first American troops landed in France in June 1917 and by the end of the month, 14,000 American soldiers had arrived. Eleven months later, over 1 million American troops were stationed in France, arriving at the rate of 10,000 a day.

About half of the US soldiers stationed in France worked on developing the French transport system so that it could move vast numbers of men and supplies quickly and efficiently. For example, they:
- enlarged French ports so that more ships could deliver men and supplies
- built over 1,600 km of railway lines
- laid over 16,000 km of telegraph and telephone cables.

The US troops that took part in the fighting played an important part in the military defeat of Germany.
- General Haig agreed to send two divisions of the recently arrived Americans to join the Allies in the second battle of the Marne in July 1918. This successfully prevented German forces taking Paris during the Ludendorff Offensive. (See page 79.)
- On 21 August 1918, over 108,000 US soldiers joined with the British Third Army in the second battle of Albert. After 2 days, over 8000 German soldiers had been captured.
- Pershing commanded the US First Army, consisting of more than 500,000 men, in the largest operation ever undertaken by American forces. Beginning on 12 September, they launched an attack on the salient created by the Ludendorff Offensive. Within 4 days, the whole salient was under Allied control. The Germans were forced to retreat.
- Between 26 September and 11 November, Pershing commanded more than 1 million American and French soldiers. Using over 300 tanks and 500 American aircraft, the troops he commanded had advanced by 32 km towards the German border by 11 November 1918.

Although the American forces played a significant role in fighting and ensuring that supply lines worked effectively, perhaps the greatest impact the US forces had on the Western Front was psychological. They were young, enthusiastic and determined. They had not had time to become depressed and tired of the war. Above all, the USA itself had an almost limitless supply of men and materials that it was prepared to use in support of the Allies. This motivated the tired Allied forces to rethink, reassess the situation and fight on.

SOURCE E

An American field hospital inside the ruins of a French church, in September 1918.

EXTRACT A

Written by a modern historian in 1978.

Once the Americans were in, the result was almost certain to be a German defeat. The United States had vast supplies of manpower and materials, far greater than the Germans could achieve. Germany fast became exhausted; so, too, did Britain and France – but they could be boosted by America.

THE HUNDRED DAYS' OFFENSIVE, 8 AUGUST–11 NOVEMBER 1918

By August 1918, the Allies were ready to go back on the offensive. The American Expeditionary Force was present in France in large numbers, and had strengthened and refreshed the Allied armies. Foch was aware that Haig commanded a highly skilled mass army, with all the artillery he needed and the backing of a strong air force. The British army had been working with new technology. This included learning how to use and interpret **aerial photography**, calculating the effect of air temperature on explosives and working out distance by recording the strength of the sound when enemy shells were fired. This meant that the British army had become a very effective fighting force. Foch therefore agreed to a British attack plan that began with an attack on Amiens.

8 AUGUST 1918, AMIENS

The Allies began their **assault** with a carefully prepared artillery barrage that knocked out all the German guns that were capable of destroying tanks. A creeping barrage followed, which travelled at the same speed as the advancing infantry and with more than 500 tanks – 92 m every 3 minutes. The attack broke through the German lines and by the end of the day, the Allies had created a gap 25 km wide south of the River Somme. By the end of the day, too, the Allies had killed, wounded or captured 48,000 enemy troops. German morale collapsed. Ludendorff described the day as 'the black day of the German army' and told the German Kaiser that Germany could not win the war. The Kaiser agreed with him.

EXTRACT B

Written by a modern historian in 2007.

The real achievement of Amiens had been the triumphant co-ordination of an all arms attack. It was the first truly modern battle. It was also the beginning of the 'hundred days' in which German forces in the West were driven back and brought so close to total destruction that on 11 November their government was forced to ask for an armistice.

SOURCE F

A cartoon published in Britain in 1918.

PUNCH, OR THE LONDON CHARIVARI.—November 13, 1918.

THE SANDS RUN OUT.

KEY TERM

Hindenburg Line a defensive line of three trench systems, built by the Germans in the winter of 1916–17

The battle of Amiens had broken the German front line. Battle after battle followed, as the Allies forced the Germans back to the **Hindenburg Line**. The old battlefields, lost to the Germans earlier in the war, were recaptured. The Allies, together with the American Expeditionary Force (see page 82) captured the Somme, successfully fought the second battle of Arras and, at the end of September, recaptured the old battlefield of Ypres where in 1917 Passchendaele had been such a disaster (see page 51).

▶ **Figure 5.2** The Hundred Days' Offensive 1918

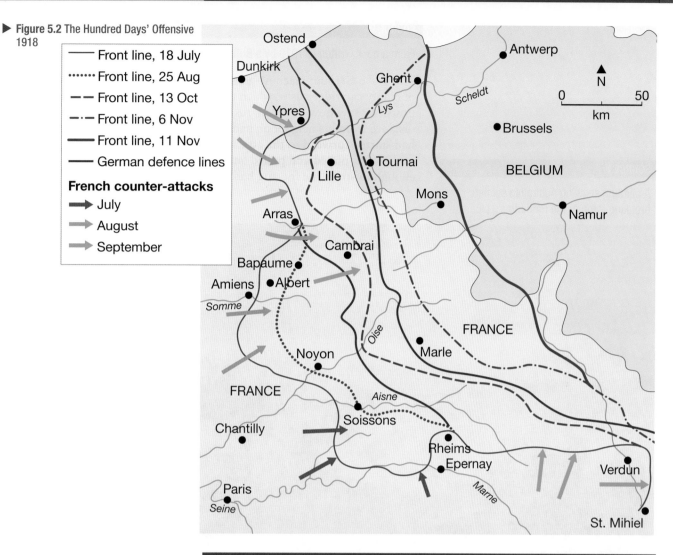

Legend:
- Front line, 18 July
- Front line, 25 Aug
- Front line, 13 Oct
- Front line, 6 Nov
- Front line, 11 Nov
- German defence lines

French counter-attacks
- July
- August
- September

SOURCE G

From the diary of a British soldier who fought in the Hundred Days' Offensive.

28 September 1918
The day's success has been astonishing; an advance of over five miles (more than in five months' bloody fighting last year). No doubt the hostile shelling has been less severe than formerly. And the enemy's infantry, behind ample defences, have not put up their usual resistance. Nevertheless, allowing for every mercy (including our smoke screens) the good leadership and drive of all our ranks from sunrise to sundown, through this bullet-swept wilderness, has been admirable, hustling the enemy off his feet.

29 September 1918
The dismal belt of land devastated by four years of war lies behind. In front, and slightly below us is spread a flat unshelled plain, crossed by winding streams and dotted with undamaged farms, hamlets and a few trees.

The main attack on the Hindenburg Line began on 29 September 1918. By 8 October, four massive offensives enabled the Allies to break through the Hindenburg Line. It was this breakthrough that forced the German High Command to accept that the war had to be ended.

SOURCE H

SOURCE H

From a book written in 1919 by a British soldier, who fought in the Hundred Days' Offensive.

The brave German machine-gunners lay dead beside their machines and piles of empty cartridge cases, which they had fired before being bayoneted at their posts. We saw how our men, rushing forward in formation, each man a good distance from his neighbour, had fallen, one here, another there, one directly he had started forward to the attack; one poor wretch had got far, but got tangled in the wire, pulled and pulled and at last had been shot; another had got near enough to strike the foe and had been shot with a revolver.

SOURCE I

A painting showing Australian soldiers breaking through the Hindenburg Line.

EXTEND YOUR KNOWLEDGE

WILFRED OWEN, 1893–1918
Wilfred Owen, who wrote the poem on page 47, was killed on 4 November 1918. He started fighting on the Western Front in January 1917 and was sent back home suffering from shell-shock. He returned to France and in October 1918 was awarded the Military Cross for bravery. He was killed while leading his men across a canal on the Western Front. The news of his death reached his parents on Armistice Day, 11 November 1918.

Throughout October, the German armies retreated through the territory they had gained in 1914. As they went, the troops abandoned large amounts of heavy equipment and supplies. This further reduced their morale and their capacity to fight back, but they never stopped fighting, even though they were in full retreat.

ARMISTICE
Realising that defeat was inevitable, the German government asked the United States to arrange an end to the fighting. Germany's allies – Bulgaria, Turkey and Austria-Hungary – had already made peace with the Allies. Inside Germany, there were riots as people starved and a deadly 'flu (**influenza**) virus spread across the country. The navy rebelled and, on 9 November, the Kaiser **abdicated** and escaped to Holland.

On 11 November 1918, in a railway carriage in the French forest of Compiegne, the Germans agreed to the Allies' terms for an armistice. They had no choice. At the 11th hour of the 11th month, 1918, the guns stopped firing. It was finished.

ACTIVITY

1 Draw a timeline 'The Allied drive to victory', starting in July and ending in November 1918. Which event do you think was the most significant? Write a sentence to explain why.

2 Read Source D. Why might an Allied soldier find it encouraging and a German soldier find it depressing?

3 Read the section 'American forces on the Western Front'. Work with a partner. One of you must represent the Americans working on building the railway lines, establishing telecommunications and expanding the French ports; the other must represent the American soldiers involved in military action. Write down, and if possible act out, an argument between the two as to who was making the most important contribution to Allied victory.

4 Look at Source F. The Kaiser is shown as worrying that Germany's time to achieve victory is running out. Find two events that could have led him to think this, and explain your choice.

5.3 THE REASONS FOR GERMANY'S DEFEAT

LEARNING OBJECTIVES

- Understand the ways in which food shortages and illness contributed to the final defeat of Germany
- Understand the ways in which political turmoil contributed to the final defeat of Germany
- Understand the reasons for the military defeat of Germany.

There is no single reason for the Allies' victory in the autumn of 1918. There are a number of factors, some more important than others, which together led to Germany's final defeat. Once the Schlieffen Plan had failed (see page 14), the war became one of attrition. The winner would be the side that could carry on the longest, and this meant carrying on in terms of manpower and supplies. Soldiers that were killed needed replacing, as did weapons that were destroyed by enemy fire or abandoned during retreats. Armies needed to be supplied with bullets, shells and food. In order for this to work well, the home government needed to be secure and well organised. It had to be able to organise its industry and agriculture so that both the fighting forces and their families left behind at home were supplied with what they needed. This would have the added benefit of keeping morale high: the soldiers at the front would feel supported and the people at home would believe that their armed forces were fighting in their best interests.

FOOD, FAMINE AND 'FLU

KEY TERM

conscript to make someone join the army, navy or air force

When the army was mobilised for war in 1914, the army took most of the horses that the farmers used for pulling ploughs, and they **conscripted** many of the farmers themselves. The army needed the horses for transporting armaments and supplies, and they needed the men to fight in the army. Then the army took large numbers of farm animals and killed them to feed the army. This meant that German agriculture became far less productive after 1914 than it had been before the war. This would not have mattered if the Schlieffen Plan had worked and the war had been a quick one. Because the Plan failed, German politicians had to organise feeding both the army and the people at home. Feeding the army came first.

Germany began to rely on importing food from European countries. However, the British naval blockade worked well. Germany could not import very much food, and it could not import nitrates (a type of chemical) that were needed, for growing better food and making explosives. Food production in Germany fell dramatically and the situation was not helped by a series of bad harvests. By 1918, there was **famine** in Germany and the people were starving. They were cold, too, as the blockade prevented adequate supplies of **coal** and other fuel from getting in to Germany.

SOURCE J

German women working on a farm towards the end of the war.

Many civilians lost faith in the ability of their government to support them. Additionally, most Germans believed their government's claim that the U-boat campaign was starving Britain and the Allies. However, when German soldiers captured British and French supply dumps during the Ludendorff Offensive (see page 78), they found them full of food – jam, coffee and white bread, for example – that they hadn't seen for a long time. This further added to the growing lack of trust in the German government.

In the summer of 1918, a severe form of 'flu affected most of the countries in the world. It spread through Germany where the people, already weakened by hunger, died in their thousands. On just one day, 1722 Berliners died from 'flu. Altogether, there were about 400,000 civilian deaths in Germany before the 'flu virus disappeared in 1919. Starving and desperate people rioted against the government that they believed had betrayed them.

EXTEND YOUR KNOWLEDGE

INFLUENZA 1918–19
About 500 million people, worldwide, were ill from 'flu, and between 40 and 50 million died from it in the years 1918–19. This was far more than the 38 million civilian and military casualties (dead and wounded) in the whole of the First World War.

POLITICAL TURMOIL

There were riots and revolts in three main centres in Germany.

- On 29 October 1918, sailors in ships of the German navy, moored on the Kiel canal, rebelled. They had heard a rumour that they were to be sent out for one last battle with the British Royal Navy. They believed that to do this would be suicidal. They refused to obey orders and joined a movement on 4 November that promised to set up soldiers' and workers' councils in rebellion against the existing government.
- In Munich on 8 November 1918, a revolutionary movement set up a Bavarian Democratic and Socialist Republic.
- In Berlin there were strikes and riots in the streets. On 9 November 1918, the Kaiser escaped to Holland and a new government was set up. Wilhelm II formally abdicated on 28 November.

SOURCE K

German workers protesting in Berlin, November 1918.

MILITARY DEFEAT

- The Ludendorff Offensive (see page 78) had stretched the German army to its limit. Arms, food and relief troops could not, where they existed, reach the front-line troops. Forced to retreat during the Allied Hundred Days' Offensive, they abandoned guns, ammunition and supplies. Morale in the army was low and hundreds of soldiers deserted.

- By the summer of 1918, the British army had learned how to combine artillery and infantry in a combined attack. Allied commanders understood how technology could be used effectively, together with a combined artillery and infantry attack. This was shown clearly at the battle of Amiens on 8 August 1918.

- Almost 2 million American troops on the Western Front gave the Allied forces a great boost. They raised morale and supported the Allies in stopping the Ludendorff Offensive and in the Allied Hundred Days' Offensive. The USA, with its vast resources of manpower and supplies, could continue to support the Allies for a long time.

- Germany's allies surrendered: Bulgaria made peace with the Allies in September 1918, Turkey in October 1918 and, on 4 November, Austria-Hungary also surrendered.

Although there were many people in Britain and France who would have liked the war to end with the Allies marching into Berlin, there was no Allied invasion of Germany. Instead, the Allies imposed a peace treaty that included making Germany accept responsibility for starting the war.

ACTIVITY

1 Study Source J. Does this source prove that the Germans were short of food? Explain your answer.
2 Work in groups of six. You are going to make a large spider diagram showing the reasons for Germany's defeat in the First World War. Two of you draw a spider diagram focusing on food, famine and 'flu; two of you draw one focusing on political troubles and two of you draw one focusing on military defeats. Put the three diagrams together, making links between them.
3 Use the giant spider diagram to answer the question, 'In considering why Germany lost the war, how important a factor were food shortages?'.
4 Select six events that happened in 1918 that were important in bringing about the Allied victory. Make connections between them to show how they worked together. You could draw this on a chart.
5 Why did the Ludendorff Offensive fail for the Germans and the Hundred Days' Offensive succeed for the Allies?
6 What was the impact on the Western Front of the USA's declaration of war on Germany?

EXAM-STYLE QUESTIONS

A03

SKILLS   ANALYSIS, ADAPTIVE LEARNING, CREATIVITY

A03   **A04**

SKILLS   CRITICAL THINKING, REASONING, DECISION MAKING, ADAPTIVE LEARNING, CREATIVITY, INNOVATION

(a) Study Sources G and H (pages 85 and 86). How far does Source G support what Source H says about the Hundred Days' Offensive?
Explain your answer.   **(8 marks)**

(b) Study Extract A (page 83). Extract A suggests that the main reason for the defeat of Germany in 1918 was the arrival of US troops in Europe.
How far do you agree with this interpretation?
Use Extracts A and B, Source F and your own knowledge to explain your answer.
    (16 marks)

HINT

(a) When asked to consider how far one source supports another, it is important to look for both agreement and disagreement. Once you have established that, you will be better placed to consider the 'extent' of support.
(b) The question asks you to use your own knowledge, so make sure you bring in some evidence that is not in the sources or the extract.

RECAP

RECALL QUIZ

1 When did the USA declare war on Germany?
2 What happened as a result of the Treaty of Brest-Litovsk (March 1917)?
3 When was the Ludendorff Offensive launched?
4 What were the specially trained German soldiers, used during the Ludendorff Offensive, called?
5 How far into France did the Ludendorff Offensive go?
6 What does AEF stand for?
7 When did the Hundred Days' Offensive begin?
8 What was the Hindenburg Line?
9 Who was in charge of the British armies during the Hundred Days' Offensive?
10 When was the armistice between Germany and the Allies signed?

CHECKPOINT

STRENGTHEN

S1 Why did the USA declare war on Germany?
S2 Re-read the information about the Ludendorff Offensive. Identify one reason for it, one event and one consequence.
S3 What was the importance of the Hindenburg Line?

CHALLENGE

C1 To what extent was the Ludendorff Offensive a success?
C2 To what extent was the battle of Amiens (8 August 1918) a turning point in 1918?
C3 Would the Allies have won the war without the intervention of the USA?

SUMMARY

- The Germans launched the Ludendorff Offensive in the spring of 1918.
- The offensive took German troops to within 65 km of Paris.
- The Germans had gone too far, too fast. Reinforcements and supplies could not keep up.
- In April 1917, the USA declared war on Germany.
- US troops improved communications in France and fought with the Allies against Germany.
- In August 1918, the Allies launched the Hundred Days' Offensive.
- The Allies used new technology to improve their tactics.
- The Allies pushed the German armies back over the Hindenburg Line into Germany.
- The German Kaiser fled to Holland and abdicated.
- Many German people died from 'flu.
- There were strikes and riots in Germany because the people were close to starvation.
- The German navy rebelled.
- Germany's allies (Bulgaria, Turkey and Austria-Hungary) surrendered.
- Germany asked the Allies for an armistice. On the 11th hour of the 11th month in 1918, the war ended.

EXAM GUIDANCE: PART (A) QUESTIONS

A01

Question to be answered: Describe **two** features of either US troop activity on the Western Front (1917–18) or the assassination of the Archduke Franz Ferdinand in 1914.
(6 marks)

1 Analysis Question 1: What is the question type testing?
In this question, you have to demonstrate that you have knowledge and understanding of the key features and characteristics of the period studied. In this particular case, it is knowledge and understanding of either US troop activity on the Western Front (1917–18) or the assassination of the Archduke. In this example, we are going to presume that the candidate has answered on US troop movement.

2 Analysis Question 2: What do I have to do to answer the question well?
Obviously you have to choose one of the two options and write about it! But it isn't just a case of writing everything you know. You have to write about two features. What are features? They are 'aspects' or 'characteristics'. We might even say that if you were allowed to put sub-headings in your answers, both features would be the sub-headings you would put.

So, in this case, you might write about the cause as a feature by saying 'US troop activity on the Western Front was because of…' or the details of the actions of the US troops by saying 'One of the actions of the US troops on the Western front was…' or the effects of US troop activity as a feature by saying 'The US troops played an important part… '.

3 Analysis Question 3: Are there any techniques I can use to make it very clear that I am doing what is needed to be successful?
This is a 6-mark question and you need to make sure you leave enough time to answer the other two questions fully (they are worth 24 marks in total). Therefore, you need to get straight into writing your answer. The question asks for two features, so it's a good idea to write two paragraphs and to begin each paragraph with phrases like 'One feature was…', 'Another feature was…'. You will get a mark for each feature you identify and up to 2 marks for giving detail to support it. This gives the maximum of 6 marks.

You have to demonstrate knowledge, so make sure you back up your paragraphs with as much detailed knowledge as you have. But remember, you are not writing an essay here. You are providing enough detail to pick up 2 extra marks on each feature you have identified.

Answer A

The US troops fought with British troops in the battle of the Marne in July 1918. They also built railways in France. They played an important part in the defeat of Germany.

What are the strengths and weaknesses of Answer A?

It doesn't have many strengths. It identifies two features (that US troops fought in the battle of the Marne in 1918, and that they built railways in France) but the final sentence (that they played an important part in the defeat of Germany) is more of an assertion than detailed support. This answer is not going to get more than 2 marks. It needs much more detail.

Answer B

One feature of US troop activity on the Western Front was that they worked with the Allied troops in helping to defeat Germany. Two divisions of Americans joined the Allies in the second battle of the Marne in July 1918 that prevented the Germans taking Paris during the Ludendorff Offensive. The following month they joined the British Third Army in the defeat of the Germans at the battle of Albert.

Another feature of US troop activity on the Western Front was the work they did on developing the French transport system. They enlarged French ports so that more troops and supplies could be landed in France; they built over 1,600 km of railway lines and laid over 16,000 km of telephone and telegraph cables.

What are the strengths and weaknesses of Answer B?

This is an excellent answer. It identifies two features (working with Allied forces and developing the French transport system). It clearly shows there are two features and provides detailed support for them both. There is no need to look for ways to improve this answer, you should just learn from it.

Challenge a friend

Use the Student Book to set a part (a) question for a friend. You could use the other option for the question above – two features of the assassination of the Archduke Franz Ferdinand. Then look at the answer. Does it do the following things?

☐ Identify two features
☐ Make it clear two features are being covered
☐ Provide 3–4 lines of detailed information to support the feature.

If it does, you can tell your friend that the answer is very good!

GLOSSARY

abdicate to give up the position of being king or queen

aerial photography photographs taken from an elevated position, often a plane

aggression the act of attacking a country, especially when that country has not attacked first

alliance an arrangement in which two or more countries agree to work together to try to change or achieve something

ally when countries agree to help or support each other in a war

ambush a sudden attack on someone by people who have been hiding and waiting for them

ammunition dump place where ammunitions are kept

amputate to cut off a limb during a medical operation

antibiotic a drug that is used to kill bacteria and cure infections

armour a metal covering on vehicles to protect them from attack

assassinate to murder an important person

assault a military attack to take control of a place controlled by the enemy

Balkan League an alliance formed between the Balkan states of Greece, Bulgaria, Serbia and Montenegro

barbed wire wire with short sharp points on it

bayonet a long knife that is fixed to the end of a rifle

blockade (naval) the surrounding of an area by ships to stop people or supplies entering or leaving

Bolshevik a supporter of the communist party at the time of the Russian Revolution in 1917

campaign a series of battles and attacks intended to achieve a particular result in a war

cannon a large heavy powerful gun used to fire heavy metal balls

casualty someone who is hurt or killed in an accident or war

cavalry the part of an army that fights on horses

chlorine a greenish-yellow gas

civilian anyone who is not a member of the military forces or the police

coal a hard black mineral that is dug out of the ground and burnt to produce heat

cockpit the place where a pilot sits in a plane

colony a country or area that is under the political control of a more powerful country, usually one that is far away

combat fighting during a war

condensed milk cow's milk from which water has been removed. It comes in tins and is long lasting

confrontation a fight or battle

constitution a set of basic laws and principles that a country or organisation is governed by

counter-attack an attack made against someone in response to their attack

cruiser a large fast ship with guns used by the navy

destroyer a small fast military ship with guns

Dogger Bank a large sandbank in a shallow area of the North Sea, about 100 km from the coast of Britain

dug-outs a shelter dug into the ground for soldiers

empire a group of countries that are all controlled by one ruler or government

entente a situation in which two or more countries have friendly relations with each other

evacuate to send people away from a dangerous place to a safe place

famine a situation in which a large number of people have little or no food for a long time

firing squad a group of soldiers whose duty is to punish prisoners by shooting and killing them

first aid simple medical treatment that is given as soon as possible to someone who is injured or who suddenly becomes ill

fleet a group of ships, or all the ships in a navy

focus to give special attention to one particular person or thing

goggles protective glasses worn by pilots

heir to the throne person who will become the next king or queen

hypnosis a state similar to sleep, in which someone's thoughts and actions can be influenced by someone else

hypothesis an explanation or theory

industrialise when a country or area develops a lot of industry for the first time

infantry soldiers who fight on foot

influenza an infectious disease that is like a very bad cold

intervention the act of becoming involved in an argument, fight or other difficult situation in order to change what happens

isolated an action, event or example that happens only once, and is not likely to happen again

loot property taken from an enemy, civilians or combatants, at a time of war

louse (pl. lice) a small insect that lives on the hair or skin of people or animals

machinery machines, especially large ones used in industry

mainland Europe the European continent

merchant navy all of a country's ships that are used for trade, not war, and the people who work on these ships

merchant ships a ship used to carry goods or passengers, rather than soldiers or military equipment

mine a type of bomb that is hidden just below the ground or under water and that explodes when it is touched

mineral a substance that is formed naturally in the earth, such as coal, salt, or gold

morale the level of confidence and positive feelings that people have

moral obligation a duty to be carried out based on a belief that it is the right thing to do

mustard gas a poisonous gas that burns the skin

nationalism love for your country and the belief that it is better than any other country

neutral a country that does not support any of the countries involved in a war

no-man's-land land between enemy trenches that was claimed by neither side

pacifist someone who believes that wars are wrong and who refuses to fight in one

patriotic having or expressing a great love of your country

peace treaty an agreement that ends a war between two or more countries

peninsula a piece of land almost completely surrounded by water

phosgene a poisonous gas

political turmoil a state of extreme unrest or unease or agitation, in relation to the government of a country

propaganda campaign an organised program that spreads information among a population to convince people to support a particular point of view

raw materials the basic materials from which a product is made

recruitment the process of finding new people to join the army, navy or air force

republic a country governed by elected representatives of the people, and led by a president, not a king or queen

revolt strong and often violent action by a lot of people against their ruler or government

riot a situation in which a large crowd of people behave in a violent and uncontrolled way, especially when they are protesting about something

salient a piece of land that juts out to form a bulge

shell-shock a type of mental illness caused by the terrible experiences of fighting in a war or battle

Slav someone who comes from Eastern or Central Europe

splendid isolation a policy of deliberately avoiding alliances to avoid being dragged into war

squadron a military force consisting of a group of aircraft or ships

stretcher a type of bed used for carrying someone who is too injured or ill to walk

submarine a ship, especially a military one, that can stay under water

suffocate to die or make someone die by preventing them from breathing

suppression to stop people from opposing the government, especially by using force

tactics the science of arranging and moving military forces in a battle

tank a heavy military vehicle that has a large gun and runs on two metal belts fitted over its wheels

telegram a message sent by telegraph, and delivered in written or printed form

Territorial Army a military force of people who train as soldiers in their free time

trigger cause something to happen

U-boat the name for German submarines, from the German word *Unterseeboten*

unification the act of combining two or more groups, countries, etc. to make a single group or country

volunteer someone who joins the army, navy, or air force without being forced to

warfare particular methods of fighting

INDEX